D1617134

TIME AND IMAGINATION

RETHINKING THEORY

TIME AND IMAGINATION

Chronotopes in Western Narrative Culture

Bart Keunen

Northwestern University Press
Evanston, Illinois

Northwestern University Press
www.nupress.northwestern.edu

Printed in the United States of America

10   9   8   7   6   5   4   3   2   1

ISBN 978-0-8101-2764-7

Library of Congress Cataloging-in-Publication Data

Keunen, Bart.
    Time and imagination : chronotopes in Western narrative culture / Bart Keunen.
        p. cm. — (Rethinking theory)
    Includes bibliographical references and index.
    Based on the author's Dutch work, Verhaal en verbeelding (Gent : Academia Press, 2007).
    ISBN 978-0-8101-2764-7 (cloth : alk. paper)
    1. Time in literature. 2. Imagination in literature. I. Title.
    PN56.T5K477 2011
    809.93384—dc22

                                                                2011011113

♾ The paper used in this publication meets the minimum requirements of the American National Standard for Information Sciences—Permanence of Paper for Printed Library Materials, ANSI Z39.48-1992.

For Yde and Leto, my daughters

Contents

Acknowledgments

This book is the culmination of many years of research, thinking, and writing that began in 1997, with my dissertation on French and German urban literature. My research led me to the idea of conceiving literary urban images as chronotopes. This idea proved to be very productive and provided the impetus for two works I wrote in Dutch, published in 2005 and 2007. These two works gave me the opportunity both to combine Mikhail Bakhtin's theory of the chronotopes with insights from contemporary narratological theory and to embed my findings into a general theory of literary imagination. This book is largely based on the second Dutch work, *Verhaal en Verbeelding (Narrative and Imagination)*, which was published by Academia Press in Ghent, thanks to the efforts of Geert Vandenbossche. Jo Smets's talent for translating my philosophical arguments into lucid English will give this book an opportunity to reach a new, wider audience. In arriving at a final draft, I have also benefited from Carol Richards's fine editorial work.

This book has been so long in the making that I have incurred a great many debts to several colleagues and friends while I was writing it. It gives me great pleasure to be able to repay them here in a symbolic, albeit brief, manner. My gratitude goes, in alphabetical order, to Jan Baetens, Nele Bemong, Lars Bernaerts, Pieter Borghart, Karel Boulart, Sascha Bru, Philippe Codde, Freddy Decreus, Michel De Dobbeleer, Luc De Droogh, Kristoffel Demoen, Katrien Demoor, Bart Eeckhout, Luc Herman, Eva Pszeniczko, Annemiek Seeuws, Ronald Soetaert, Steven Tötösy, Pieter Uyttenhove, Rik Van Gorp, Laurence van Nuijs, Sofie Verraest, Bart Verschaffel, Kries Versluys, and Raymond Vervliet.

I would also like to extend my thanks to the students of my Comparative Literature courses at Ghent University. For nearly four years and through approximately 1,200 case studies, they provided me with ample evidence about readers' attitudes toward plot dynamics, moral reasoning, and imaginative stimuli. Their contribution to my perspective on the chronotopic imagination has been invaluable.

My greatest debt as a scholar, however, is to Gary Saul Morson, who showed me, and encouraged me to embrace fully, the potential of a more philosophically oriented approach to literary imagination. I thank him for being a constant inspiration and, most of all, for his willingness and ability to say the right words at the right moment, in true kaironomic fashion.

TIME AND IMAGINATION

Introduction:
Narrative Imagination

I climb'd the dark brow of the mighty Helvellyn,
Lakes and mountains beneath me gleam'd misty and white,
All was still, save by fits, when the eagle was yelling,
And starting around me the echoes replied.

Walter Scott, "Helvellyn"

There are two avenues leading toward literary theory: one invites us to the close-up of literary language; the other opens up the panorama of narrative imagination. At the beginning of the latter avenue, arguably the more attractive and important one, a signpost says: possible dead end. After all, if literary theory is first and foremost the study of narrative imagination, then the subject of the conversation literary theorists and critics engage in must strike any scientific explorer as very vague and elusive. What is there to make of a subject that consists of realities possessing no other existential basis than the realm of mental representations formed by readers and narrators? It is true that by studying texts and language one could attempt to establish a systematized conversation about these mental images. However, as a scientific discipline, the insights provided by literary theory must inevitably be into a world of highly movable images, a world that originates and exists solely in the brain of those participating in narrative exchanges. It is easy to imagine a dead end in such an endeavor. We can get a good idea of the difficulties that lie ahead for any literary theorist taking the second avenue in a passage from *The Concept of Mind* by the English philosopher Gilbert Ryle. While trying to explain the distinction between images of perception and images of imagination, Ryle refers to the recollected (and therefore imagined) perception of the mountain Helvellyn in England's Lake District:

> Seeing Helvellyn in one's mind's eye does not entail, what seeing Helvellyn and seeing snapshots of Helvellyn entail, the having of visual sensations. It does involve the thought of having a view of Helvellyn and it is therefore a more sophisticated operation than that of having a view of Helvellyn. (1968, 255)

In this book I choose the second avenue, the difficult path—up the elusive mountain, so to speak. I refuse to believe in dead ends and wish to propose a theory of narrative imagination, construing it as an attempt to describe the sophisticated nature of imagination. In the process of describing narrative imagination, I even plan to unveil to some extent its very own systematics.

Literary language will no doubt be badly served by this purpose. The object of my attention primarily resides in the effects of literary language (in the state of consciousness of readers and narrators) and in the description of these effects. The actual signs emitted by the medium—text or, not infrequently, cinematic images—and intended to generate mental images will "merely" be of auxiliary importance. It was clear from the start that taking the second avenue really means ignoring the signs.

Stories are told with *imaginal images* that lack the precision and unambiguous quality of perceptual images. Consequently, I will have to demonstrate that there are invariants in narrative imagination. Just as the psychology of perception teaches us about invariants occurring in the perception of the empirical world, this book too will teach that in narrative imagination certain rules regarding invariants exist. In the course of evolution, the empirical world has forced us human beings toward strategies of knowledge that are only efficient insofar as they constitute systematized and solidly organized operations. In order to survive, the human species has had to bend its cutting-edge perceptual apparatus into a more abstract thinking device. We have learned to employ objects of knowledge that indeed may have their basis in perception but nonetheless constitute generalizations of this perceptual knowledge. Therefore, generally speaking, narrative imagination can be said to entail a form of thought of its very own. In exactly the same way as with scientific knowledge, a series of judgments is expressed about the world on the basis of empirical evidence. Recent psychological theories even assert that this imaginal form of thought that establishes itself by way of stories is to a large extent equivalent to the more abstract forms found in scientific knowledge. The cognitive scientist Jerome Bruner, in his essay "The Narrative Construction of Reality" (1991) and his book *Actual Minds, Possible Worlds* (1986), makes a comparative analysis of the two ways of knowing applied by human beings in their attempts to gain a better understanding of their world. The first, scientific knowledge, is characterized by logical relationships between the epistemic units. The elements of a scientific discourse are logical propositions, inferences deriving a causal effect from a fact and designating the process by formulating a law about it. These abstract laws lead to methodical knowledge about the processes in the world. For this reason, Bruner calls the scientific form of thought the basis for paradigmatic knowledge. It proposes paradigms in order to be able to understand invariant data. Complementing this form of thought is *narrative thought*, which operates by way of more concrete data. The building blocks of narratives do not consist of logical proofs or empirical observations but of consecutive actions and states of things. At the heart of this form of reasoning are mental images that are interconnected on the basis of spontaneous expectations. For example, when we imagine a couple in love, the expectation arises that they will exchange intimacies. The purpose of these two ways of thinking is, in fact, exactly the same, that is, to bring up processes and map the expectations about the ways in which these processes will evolve. Be that as it may, there is a difference in the material used in acquiring the knowledge. In the first case, the building blocks are empirical data that need to be isolated—for example, in a laboratory. In the second case, the laboratory is construed of *imaginal* processes conferring dynamics on the images of a fictional world.

Narrative imagination and abstract-logical reasoning are two strategies that purport to render a continually changing reality understandable. It should be noted that abstract knowledge is not superior to imaginal knowledge. Psychologists of memory go so far as to say that it is the other way around, that thought by way of images is in some aspects more efficient than abstract-logical thought. Images are not merely the imprints of reality on the brain. Keeping in mind Ryle's words, we should be aware of the fact that they always involve some sort of informational transfer or complex processes of thought. As a matter of fact, memory could be used more efficiently if information were transferred by images.[1] A second consideration for asserting the importance of images as an object of scientific inquiry is the fact that they go hand in hand with our capacity to make value judgments. One of the members of the Russian Bakhtin Circle, for example, puts it as follows:

> It seems that we perceive the value of an object together with its being, as one of its qualities; in the same way, for example, we sense the value of the sun together with its warmth and light. And thus all phenomena of being which surround us are fused together with our evaluations of them. (Voloshinov 1983, 13)

Images, therefore, are complex carriers of information, colored by judgments. These qualities a fortiori apply to narrative imagination, to the moving and interconnected images we encounter in narratives. Fiction is able to creatively transform the images that are available to us from perception and from memory; it assimilates those images in a series of narrative processes that enable us to picture for ourselves a *world-in-motion*. As a result the images gain in complexity and evaluative force. As I have said before, narrative imagination constitutes a form of knowledge. It is a "creating" knowledge, as Ferdinand Alquié expresses it: "It represents future situations, or pure phantasm; it discovers; it invents" (Alquié 1939, 266).[2] In his *Leçons de philosophie* (*Lessons in Philosophy*), Alquié, one of Gilles Deleuze's mentors, stresses that the imaginative force is so much more than the ability to represent images. He does not hesitate to claim that it represents the human brain's most vital capability:

> The power of invention that resides in us relates not only to combinations of images but also to ideas, judgments. Consequently, "imagination" should be understood as every operational thought that contemplates or combines representative materials. Indeed, imagination is nothing other than thought itself. (Alquié 1939, 266)[3]

With purely intellectual means, narrative imagination creates systematic knowledge about changes in the world. It is a laboratory in which the changes are staged, in which the occurrences in our world are explored in order to better understand them, and perhaps even correct them, in life outside of literature. Let us take this somewhat further.

The observations made by Ryle, Bruner, and Alquié may have shown narrative imagination to be a reality that distinguishes itself from perception and logic, yet this does not reveal anything about the way in which this reality ought to be studied. Classical narratology has little to offer in terms of methodological support. Narratology studies the textual invariants of a narrative by distinguishing, for example, between different rhetorical strategies involved in putting the text on paper (chronological order of time, narrator's perspective) and retracing the ways in which these strategies order the events in a text. Questions pertaining to the imaginal quality of the texts and the events represented in them, however, are not considered.

Nevertheless, in the last few years more recent narratological theories have increasingly made such questions the focus of their attention. Whereas in the initial years of its existence narratology was a science of texts, today texts are increasingly read as cultural objects that acquire meaning through numerous mental operations. Postclassical narratology—to use an appropriate term coined by Luc Herman and Bart Vervaeck (2005)—is occupied with the possible worlds communicated through narratives (Eco 1989, Ryan 1991, Pavel 1986, Dolezel 1979). Reception studies, for their part, proceed from the assumption that narratives apply strategies that aim to stimulate the reader's imagination. Film theory has witnessed the same evolution, though in a shorter interval of time. The first attempts at writing a narratology of the cinematic image avidly exhausted the semiotic stock of analytical tools (see, for example, Christian Metz). Since the publication of Deleuze's *Cinéma 1*, an increasing number of film theorists have come to the conclusion that films derive their meaning from processes of consciousness that cannot simply be deduced from the structure of the cinematic or imaginal language itself (assuming, of course, that cinema can best be studied as a "language").

One of the pioneers of narrative imagination research is the literary historian Mikhail Bakhtin. The inquiry conducted in this book is an attempt to fit the Russian literary theorist's insights, which to this day have been insufficiently studied, into a systematic theory. Drawing on insights from postclassical narratologists (Umberto Eco and David Herman, as well as Jurij Lotman, who in many aspects can also be labeled "postclassical"), I will scrutinize one of the key concepts in Bakhtin's thought: the chronotope. By using the concept of chronotope, the vague notion of "mental image" immediately proves to be more workable.[4] If narrative images are considered as mental representations that receive order from time (*chronos*) and space (*topos*), then it may be possible to describe a number of laws of narrative imagination. If a number of invariants or basic forms of narrative imagination can be discovered, then this, in turn, opens up the possibility of formulating a number of combination rules pertaining to these basic forms. As stated before, in the same way that psychologists of perception discover invariants in the perceptual strategies of a human being (the figure-background law of Gestalt psychology, for instance), we can perhaps map some elementary strategies of the human imagination by relying on Bakhtin's help.

In Bakhtin's view, the building blocks of a narrative are not primarily constituted by words and sentences (or, in the case of cinema, by rays of light capturing an image on a frame of film) but by imaginal entities. In his most commanding essay on this subject, "Forms of Time and of the Chronotope in the Novel" (1937–38), Bakhtin states in a concise yet polemical way: "Any and every literary image is chronotopic. Language, as a treasure-house of images, is fundamentally chronotopic" (1981a, 251). In his postformalist perspective, the imaginal reality generated by narrative chronotopes does not constitute only a textual form. Furthermore, it certainly cannot be reduced to mere narrative technique. For Bakhtin, the narrative images are of the same order as they are for Bruner and Alquié. Inasmuch as they are imaginal constructs, they do not belong to the text, as such, but instead represent forms of cognition; however, this does not entail that narrative images are unreal. Quite the opposite is true: they are "forms of the most immediate reality" (Bakhtin 1981a, 85; Morson and Emerson 1990, 367; Holquist 1990, 151). Time and space are indeed narratological phenomena. Time can be studied by means of Gérard Genette's concepts (analepsis, prolepsis, duration, frequency, order in story, and discourse time, etc.), and space is realized in the text by means of textually describable focalizations. Nevertheless, this is not the reason why people consume stories:

First and foremost, we experience [chronotopes] in the external material being of the work and in its purely external composition. But this material of the work is not dead, it is speaking, signifying (it involves signs); we not only see and perceive it but in it we can hear voices. . . . The text as such never appears as a dead thing; beginning with any text—and sometimes passing through a lengthy series of mediating links—we always arrive, in the final analysis, at the human voice, which is to say we come up against the human being. (Bakhtin 1981a, 252–53)

In other words, the concept of the chronotope must be connected with the human voice or with the agency behind the voice: the human imagination. In order to explicate the imaginal reality hiding behind a narrator's voice, we should focus on those laws of the imagination that wholly involve time and space. Narrative imagination, after all, pictures those situations that possess spatial and temporal coordinates. Additionally, situations in narrative imagination change in space and time.

Observers like to stress that Bakhtin was influenced by Immanuel Kant's idea of human knowledge arising from psychological (transcendental) operations in which spatial categories and time are employed. Time and space, Michael Holquist states, are essential building blocks of human perception (1990, 115), and for this reason, they return in the "perceiving" of literary images. However, as I pointed out in the previous paragraphs, there is a big difference between perceptual images and narrative images. Their experiential structure may run parallel, but, essentially, two different forms of mental imaging are involved. In my opinion, Bakhtin presents himself as a specialist of narrative imagination, of the spatial-temporal patterns specific to narratives, patterns that render change understandable. Furthermore, Bakhtin, unlike Kant, is interested only in the a posteriori conditions of experience rather than in the a priori conditions. This interest betrays a kinship with Deleuze, who with his transcendental empiricism also started a quest for the laws that characterize the effects of our experience—the laws of the images in human imagination. The origin of experience in time and space is not what interests Bakhtin; instead, he is interested in the way in which the *effects* of experience are ordered by means of time and space. Hence, I would like to state that for Bakhtin chronotopes are synonymous with the effects of imagination. The objects of inquiry in the study of chronotopes are those effects of imagination the world calls forth in a writer before and while he develops them into a text, and those effects of imagination called forth by a story while watching a film or reading. Bakhtin was the first literary theorist who attempted to map these effects.[5] He succeeded in giving the initial impetus to a *grammar of imagination*. In this book, the grammar hidden in Bakhtin's work will be reconstructed according to the following outline.

Initially, I will search for the building blocks of narrative imagination; depending on the level of abstraction of the narrative image, I distinguish different types of narrative imagination. The images appear to have time and space as (inextricably linked) coordinates. Yet the spatial component is featured intermittently, alternating between a more abstract and a more concrete fashion, thus creating clear differences in level. I will examine the chronotopes at three levels, distinguishing between action-space chronotopes, plot-space chronotopes, and worldview chronotopes. A chronotope can, of course, relate to an event in a space that can be visualized (a chase in a horror story, for example, is an action-space chronotope). It can render a development in time observable within the abstract totality of the fictional world (time and space are conjoined in what Lotman, implicitly commenting on Bakhtin, has called "the plot-space"). Finally, a chronotope can be concerned with an abstract philosophical representation about the moral implications of the depicted events, pertaining to the history of mankind or perhaps even to the order in God's creational plan (that is, a worldview chronotope).[6] Remarkably, stories seem to stimulate our imagination at each of these three levels. Knowing this, a successful narrator usually strives to inject some thrills at all three levels.

The first chapter of this book is dedicated to this syntax of narrative imagination, to the interactions and the peculiarities of the different degrees of imagination in a narrative. The second chapter, building on the first, makes an inventory of the imaginal invariants that occur at every level of chronotopic imagination. At the level of the action-space chronotope, the equilibrium and conflict chronotopes seem to be the most notable invariants; at the level of the plot-space chronotope, a fundamental distinction exists between teleological and dialogical chronotopes. The image of a peaceful, small village (equilibrium chronotope) is very different from the representation of pirates causing a couple in love to separate (conflict chronotope), just as the development of a target-driven, measured plot (teleological chronotope) contrasts with a network of relationships and tension between psychological situations that are possibly linked to characters or groups of characters (dialogical chronotope).

Time is the main criterion for distinguishing between types of action-spaces and plot-spaces. Within each of the levels further subdivisions can be made by using concepts of time: equilibrium and conflict, for example, seem to be closely tied to concepts of time such as repetition and chance. Imaginal constructs are teleological and dialogical on the basis of the role played respectively by the finishing moment (the eschaton) and the deciding moment (the kairos) in the plot construction. The fact that time is such an important criterion is largely explained by extra-narrative reasons. To a considerable extent, narrative imagination follows the same lines within and outside of literature. Thus, a clear connection can be observed between the plot pattern of a fictional world and the specific philosophical world construction outside of the narrative. Whenever narratives share a specific composition, this also frequently seems to be connected with the common worldview that hides behind the fictional world. In Bakhtin studies, this connection is represented as follows: "Since authors model whole worlds, they are ineluctably forced to employ the organizing categories of the worlds that they themselves inhabit" (Clark and Holquist 1984, 278). Worldviews and their influence on genres will be briefly discussed when I talk about chronotope types in chapter 2, but this merely anticipates the fact that they constitute the crux of a separate third chapter. In this third chapter, I will examine which genre patterns can be derived from the general observations. Within a teleological chronotope, different variants are possible depending on the position of the conflict chronotope within the whole. The position of the chronotope profoundly determines the development of time: the representation of a fictional world in which the conflict is pressed between two images of equilibrium (a mission chronotope) will be distinguished from the regeneration chronotope (a representation in which the narrative ends in a state of equilibrium after a series of conflicts) and from the degradation chronotope (a tragic image in which the loss of equilibrium is the center of attention). As far as dialogical chronotopes are concerned, a distinction will be introduced on the basis of differences in the network of narrative components. In these different networks, characters experience tragic moments (of degradation), or regenerate, or possess both components equally. I will designate these variants respectively as tragic, comic, and tragicomic chronotopes.

This comprehensive analysis will be the basis for assessing whether the basic intuitions regarding imagination and the conjoint presence of temporal and spatial concepts with their varying levels will lead to new insights in the field of narrative theory. In particular, these may pertain to (1) views on the nature of narrative communication (work, audience, and creator each construct the world of narrative imagination in their own way); (2) construction of literary texts; (3) the intertextual relationships between narratives (some motifs are very powerful temporal-spatial images that travel through narrative culture and continue to generate new variations); (4) the imaginal invariants that emerge with a group of texts (the narrative culture's genres rely on temporal and spatial patterns); and finally, (5) the part played by imagination in the strategies adopted by human beings to gain a better understanding of their world (the choice of a particular time and space frequently correlates with ideological presuppositions).

In order to come up with an answer to these questions, I need to gain a clear understanding of the very nature and power of imaginal constructs. Decades have passed since semiotic narratology or structuralist literary theory first decided to put language above imagination. It is high time—and in this I would like to follow the path inaugurated by Thomas Pavel in the introduction to his *Fictional Worlds*— to redress the balance and put imagination at the same level as language.

1

The Building Blocks of Narrative Imagination

Time as the Cornerstone of Narrative Imagination

The theory of imagination developed by Bakhtin significantly differs from traditional attempts to conceptualize narrative imagination. Neither formalist-structuralist theory nor hermeneutical or philological methodology met with his approval. For decades formalists and structuralists, justifiably dissatisfied with literary scholars caught up in theories about obscure entities like "themes," "mentalities," and "intentions," have been going out of their way to provide some scientific basis to the study of narrative imagination. In view of this scientific approach, they believed textual material to be the most fruitful object of inquiry. Bakhtin, on the contrary, claimed that the raw material of narratives consisted in mental images. He refused to have faith in the core tenet of Russian Formalism, that is, the belief that the imaginal realm could be mapped by describing the means of expression. His postformalist approach, however, deviates from traditional hermeneutical research (to the same extent as thematology and the history of mentalities) because in his view it is simply impossible to reduce narrative imagination to meanings abstracted from narrative images.

The German *Motiv- und Stoffgeschichte* (history of motifs and themes; Elisabeth Frenzel and Horst Daemmrich) and the thematological school of French comparativism (Raymond Trousson and the Genevian Thematological School around Georges Poulet and Jean Starobinski) tried to explain narrative imagination by using concepts such as theme and motif. The major flaw of these theories is exactly their method of abstracting narrative images from concepts and subsequently limiting the analysis to a comparison of these concepts. It is true that some progress was made in gaining insights into the intertextual relationships between narratives from different periods and linguistic regions, yet nothing whatsoever was learned about the experiences evoked by these sorts of images or even about the experiences that precede them. Bakhtin's methodological attitude differs from any such thematological enterprise. Abstract themes, such as love, grief, or death, he states, are like parasites attached to narrative imagination and to the experiences that take shape through these narratives: "All the novel's abstract elements . . . gravitate toward the chronotope and through it take on flesh and blood, permitting the imaging power of art to do its work" (Bakhtin 1981a, 250).

Another problem with thematology is that it is far more interested in establishing a catalogue of literary images than in understanding the cognitive or mental processes that lie behind narrative imagination. Thematologists are collectors of images, for example, images about love (the motif of the double suicide, the Romeo and Juliet theme), and comment on their diffusion and impact. These typologies are not only fairly sterile but also fail to provide any insight into literary history. On the contrary, in most cases of traditional thematological studies a tendency toward universalism is rampant, as though the theorists wanted to trace the eternal stories of mankind. Thematic catalogues offer no help at all in a scientific attempt to locate the historical roots of literary images. By using thematic catalogues, we fail to address the most important issues about narrative culture: what is the reason that love takes on the meaning of "ever-lasting" in Greek adventure novels but in Balzacian literature designates a struggle determined by fate? Why does the epic novel sing the praises of universal values while the hero in a picaresque novel is the prisoner of a contingent world? For us to be able to interpret themes, Bakhtin says, we must have a sound grasp of the strategies of imagination that exist in a given period. To use the words of Gary Saul Morson and Caryl Emerson: "for us to understand . . . meanings, they must reach us; they must pass through the gates of the chronotope" (1990, 432).

TIME AS/IS ACTION

If we are to give a thorough account of a narrative's thematic structure, then we must first attend to the study of the way in which images are created in narratives. The basis for this methodological operation is the perception that a narrative shows a world-in-motion. Narratives bring up interesting evolutions and processes, and in doing so, they make use of images that are equally characterized by change; a narrative's string of events constitutes "moving images." In this sense, time is the cornerstone of a chronotopic image, the basis of a construction of narrative imagination. Perceptual images (that arise, for instance, from contemplating or photographically reproducing a landscape) or imagined objects (the face of an absent loved one) can perfectly exist without any development of time. A *story*, by contrast, only deserves to be told (see Herman's concept of "tellability") if some form of process is involved. A narrative is only interesting inasmuch as it tells of an event that is relevant for the recipient—a meaningful action, a changing mood, the confirmation of a moral value, or the evolution of an opinion. Events, in other words, constitute the core of narrative imagination.[1]

This is the reason why philosophers who direct their attentions to narrative theory stress the fact that "time" represents the heart of narrative art, the heart of the art of storytelling. In *Temps et récit* (*Time and Narrative*), Paul Ricoeur states that fictional narratives only become narratives when they focus on creating a "mimesis of action" (1984, 290). Following Aristotle, he believes that even stylistically premature narratives constitute narratives as soon as they depict actions and processes, though any narrative evidently is dependent upon language and style. Indeed, Aristotle claims that the poet "should be the maker of plots rather than of verses; since he is a poet because he imitates, and what he imitates are actions" (1929, 51b27). Therefore, the motor behind the constructions of narrative imagination is human action. In fact, only very rarely do we encounter a narrative in which the source of change assumes a nonhuman form.[2]

Consequently, if action can be called the cornerstone of narrativity, time can be called the essential component of telling a story. In addition, this perspective turns chronotopes into the most fundamental entities in the study of narrative imagination.[3] A chronotope is an imaginal construct or entity representing a temporal process that occurs in a spatial situation. It is exactly because of the fact that every activity, every development of time, is expressed through spatial changes that we should consider chronotopes to be the essence of narratives.

This, as a matter of fact, applies to all narrative media. Cinematic images, for example, are subject to the chronotopic nature of narrative imagination. Even if the spatial element leaves very little to the imagination (everything is mechanically captured by the film camera), it is nonetheless necessary for a spectator to put the events through a mental operation. In cinema, processes of time preserve their status as the cornerstone of narrative imagination. It is no coincidence that editing is the key operation in cinema's aesthetics. Though cinematic images may seem to have little appeal to the imagination, they still exhibit a highly imaginative power by way of the plot's structure. Reality is different from cinema because the sequences of images are staged by the imagination. Reality comes alive in a specific structure through the filmmaker's imagination. Apart from this, films are chronotopic because they are the realization, both on a spatial and a temporal level, of the effects of imagination experienced by the filmmaker. Sets and lighting are adjusted in ways that allow the filmmaker to express a specific reality of imagination. The spectators are offered little room for personally specifying the cinematic images because the camera does this for them, yet through the style of directing, handling the camera, and editing, the filmmaker offers a concrete, realized form of the narrative in the film in a way his or her imagination considers it to be possible. The narrative told by the filmmaker possesses a dynamic imaginal structure that needs to be decoded by the spectators if they are to gain any insight into the narrative.

In narrative texts that work with verbal tools, such as literary narratives, the dynamics of the chronotope need to be realized in a different way. As banal as this may seem, one of the primary means to this end is the use of verbs. In *Mille Plateaux*, Deleuze notes that verbs represent the heart of an event. In the "becoming" of a situation, the image-in-motion is expressed in the verb (Deleuze and Guattari 1980, 263). Apart from verbs, narratives apply temporal indicators that point out the leading moments in the narrative processes. Indicators such as "suddenly," "exactly on time," "at that moment," and "one day later," among others, give rhythm to adventurous events and tell us something about the contingency of the actions occurring in the fictional world. Other indicators are related to conceptions of time in which chance hardly has any part to play: "on a beautiful Sunday afternoon" or "they lived happily ever after." By means of these temporal indicators, a situation in equilibrium is expressed. As we will see, the time of a love affair or of a creational myth is entirely constructed by means of reiterating processes that generate an image of equilibrium. Through the staging of seasons and natural cycles, a narrator fully subsumes a narrative within themes of repetition and regularity.

TIME AS/IS PLOT
The building blocks of narratives are moving images, which can be interpreted and designated as stable entities (the duel or the fight, for example). Nonetheless, as mental constructs, they wholly incorporate a "becoming."

We can also observe the way in which narratives depict changes on the level of the rounded-off narrative. The well-established notion of plot represents a temporal pattern that guarantees the narrators, the audience, and the text itself the rational order of the narrative.[4] E. M. Forster, Ricoeur, and Peter Brooks also detect in a plot a logical whole that can turn a chain of events into a narrative (Richardson 2005, 353). Plot, in other words, clearly involves mental activity. For this reason, Dame Gillian Beer considers plot mechanisms to be the "organizing principles of . . . thinking" (1983, 47). Ricoeur, in turn, reserves the term "emplotment" for the reflexive activity behind the narrative, for introducing subdivisions in and applying structures to a narrative. For Ricoeur (1984), all instances of narrative art involve some kind of reflection. In consuming a narrative, we reflect upon a world-in-motion and represent this world as a totality. We practice, in other words, *totalizing visualization*. In the images that result from this operation, the beginning and end of a narrative are brought together, while recollected fragments in the middle function as a chain of elements connecting beginning and end. Adventurous fairytale heroes depart from home to solve problems in inhospitable regions, only to arrive safely home again after their adventures. This example of what I will call a teleological chronotope demonstrates that the changing spatial situation is accompanied by a temporal process: an initial situation gradually transforms into a new shape and ultimately leads to an end situation, which sharply contrasts with the middle part. This process of totalization is already active during the reception of the narrative. Even if we do not know the ending yet and have not passed through all episodes, we can still gather a representation of the whole. Anticipation, for that matter, belongs to the core of the reception process.

Another form of totalizing visualization is the imaginal construct of a network of characters (consider, for example, the relationships between Madame Bovary and her lovers) or the imaginal representation of the tension in the fundamental relationship between a character and his environment (for example, between Alfred Döblin's Franz Biberkopf and all of the actors he is confronted with in Berlin). This type of imaginal construction could be labeled as a dialogical chronotope—a network of singular time events or kairos moments.

TIME IN IMPLICIT WORLDVIEWS

The images-in-motion and worlds-in-motion are what makes it possible for us to call narratives, as Frank Kermode aptly expresses it, "fictive models of the temporal world" (1968, 54). Time can be connected not only to actions and plot-spaces but also to worldviews. The world-in-motion narrative, after all, obeys certain genre conventions that are in turn influenced by general views of time and space. Consider a writer of a story that is ruled by the time of adventures, or in which adventures lead to a satisfying happy ending. It is obvious that this writer chooses a different concept of time than, for example, a writer of tragedies or biographies. In an adventure story, time's impact on heroic actions is great, yet it is small or nonexistent on philosophical meditations or the biographic accounts of the principal characters. Adventure narratives are particularly proficient in establishing characters in an unrealistic manner because the conception of time does not allow realism. When Ulysses' long journey draws to a close, he has not changed a bit: setting foot on Ithaca, he requires Athena's help to take on the guise of an old man. Homer is so intently focused on the time of adventure that he does not bother to represent his hero, who has wandered the face of the earth for twenty years, as twenty years older. A biographer, by contrast, can be set to trace signs of decay on a scale of months. The same contrast exists between modern "realistic" stories and the myth-infused epics of antiquity. The backdrop of *Le rouge et le noir* (*The Red and the Black*) is the history of the French Revolution and the Restoration, while in the Iliad it is the eternal world of the Olympic gods. Worldviews (whether they are political or mythical) no longer belong to the narrative but involve ideological or philosophical inferences that originate with the recipient (see Eco's view on possible worlds in *Lector in fabula*).

The impact of worldviews also demonstrates that the images offered in narrative invariably comment on a specific type of experience. Evaluating human experience presupposes an adequate concept of time. Through our examination of time, we are tracing the ways in which the storytelling human animal reacts to experiences (the experience of chance, the experience of the relativity of a project) and how he or she attempts to get a grip on these experiences by constructing fictional representations. Literary historians, therefore, have an important part to play in the study of narrative imagination. By analyzing the differences in plot structure and the contrasts between genres on the imaginal level, we can gain an idea of the experiential invariables that are active in a culture and of the evolution that affects cultural experiences.

The Narrative Space

As fundamental as concepts of time may be for an analysis of narrative imagination, images are still not adequately describable without taking into account the spatial embedding of temporal processes. Nevertheless, only the temporal dimension is taken into consideration in many narrative theories. Aristotle famously argued that plot and mimesis (the depiction of action) were essentially sufficient to define narrative art. In the same way, Ricoeur thought that only time was needed to define the narrative identity of man. Most theorists do not share our view of narrative imagination as an imaginal entity in the broadest sense of the phrase (as a temporal and spatial given). They merely discuss plot patterns or the abstract order that provides structure to the succession of images. In my opinion, however, this goes against the commonsense views of the narrative space and runs counter to more than one narratological and empirical theory. It is hard to see how anyone can ignore the fact that narratives are stored in memory by means of spatial images. Bruno Hillebrand is right to point out that we first remember a setting when we are plumbing the depths of memory while attempting to call a fictional text to mind (1971, 418). Intuitions of this kind have led some narrative theorists to define space as a fundamental dimension of narrative imagination. Lotman, for example, holds that "the iconic principle and a graphical quality are wholly peculiar to verbal models" (1977, 217). Other narratologists no doubt share his thoughts when he emphasizes that the reception of a text is accompanied by the generation of visual denotata (Lotman 1977, 55; Bal 1978, 49). Although classical narratology makes room for examining spatiality, it would be presumptuous to say that it is genuinely concerned with the spatial component of the imagination.

Two problems loom large over many theories regarding literary space. The first is that the narrative space in these theories is never interpreted in its process-based and temporal aspects. The space is indeed never analyzed as a "moving" space. As a result, time in these theories is never more than a dimension next to the spatial dimension. In Herman's recent narratological work, however, temporality is connected with spatiality; he mentions "a process of cognitive mapping that assigns referents not merely a temporal but a spatiotemporal position in the storyworld" (2002, 297). Here, Herman's analysis nearly approaches the Bakhtinian theory of imagination.[5] The second problem that keeps narratological studies from fully assuming a theory of imagination is the fact that the different levels of abstraction through which narrative imagination realizes the spatial dimension are insufficiently taken into consideration.[6] Before discussing the interweaving of time and space, I would like to further explain these different stages or levels of abstraction.

On the basis of the three forms of spatiality, I wish to delineate three types of chronotopes: the first type consists of those imaginal constructs that cause mimetic effects in the recipient's imagination; the second type involves constructs based on a representation of the abstract spaces in which the narrated events unfold; the third type concerns constructs of imagination that are solely aimed at visualizing abstract ideas: the worldviews. Clearly, it is no coincidence that these three levels correspond to the three levels of time discussed in the previous section. The narrative space shifts its shape depending on how it is established within the context of concrete actions, abstract plot developments, and philosophical worldviews. In this way, three forms of imagination or chronotopy arise: action-space chronotopes, plot-space chronotopes, and worldview chronotopes.

THE VISUAL REPRESENTATION OF SPACE

The spaces we remember when calling to mind a book (and this also applies to recollecting a film) are not always equally concrete. The spatiality of mental images is invariably abstract. We must keep in mind what Ryle correctly observed: perceiving a mountain or a photographic reproduction of a mountain is entirely different from imagining one. Cognitive psychologist J. R. Anderson points out that even in the case of representations of empirical objects we cannot assert that the mental image unambiguously reflects those objects. An imagined object always implies a colored view of that object. It is never identical to a visual perception of the object because the brain tends to represent things schematically:

> Although many people report experiences of visualizing objects in imagery tasks, an image does not seem to be a mental picture in the head. It differs from a picture in that it is not tied to the visual modality, it is not precise and can be distorted, and it is segmented into meaningful pieces. (Anderson 1980, 63)

When readers have their minds on visual denotata (see Lotman), this does not in the least imply that they are experiencing a real perception. In many cases, when we think of a concrete object, we merely create a schematic form, which is far from exact. In our imagination, a drawing of a rectangle divided into four parts by a cross-shaped construction can readily be associated with the idea of a window. Imagination often operates by means of *pars pro toto*: a few meaningful segments of an object are sufficient to make us recognize and designate an image.

The art of caricature drawing and certainly of comic strips fully exploits this type of imaginative ability. The perception of objects, in other words, is always schematic, offering the perceiver a certain amount of freedom. This is a fortiori the case for purely mental images. We can perfectly imagine a unicorn without ever having seen one. The vagueness of the image is even stronger as soon as the mental moving images of narrative imagination are engaged. The moving images are indeed characterized by schematization and reductionism at several instances of the mental processing.

Verbal narratives tend to suffer greatly from the schematic reductionism that characterizes imagined objects because they simply lack the means for visualizing spatial objects. Not all spatial objects can be represented in a text. That is why— or, more appropriately, this is *where*—the power of suggestion comes into the picture.[7] Literary texts appeal to spatial indicators ("Petersburg," "Nevski Prospect," "mansion," "room," "on the table") to generate spatial images in readers' minds. These are certainly not limited to geographical indications or descriptions of the setting in which the plot actions take place. The spatial dimension also includes, for example, the physiological traits of characters; as we shall see, some characters can even be visualized as part of the spatial backdrop. Texts also resort to extensive descriptions to create an illusion of spatiality. By fusing objects (that is, juxtaposing elements that in reality "happen" simultaneously), the narrative text suggests the coordinates and dimensions of the space the reader must call to mind. In the process, the text reduces the spatial situation to a structure:

> A spatial object is characterized by its being complete, full, and existing simultaneously. In the attempt to give verbal expression to the structure of such an object, the object must first lose some of its "completeness," since it is impossible to give an identical expression to all its parts and aspects. . . . Language cannot give full expression to the spatial existence of any object. (Zoran 1984, 313)

In a narrative, the spatial situation is always a kind of matrix: the character is situated in this or that spatial environment (a room related to a house, a street, a city, and an even larger topographical space), moves around (from the southern side to the northern side of the room), and reaches for objects (an apple on the table). It is this matrix that is represented in a person's narrative imagination. Lotman has mapped this very clearly in *The Structure of the Artistic Text*, where he quotes A. D. Aleksandrov to define literary spatial images as simulations of relationships. Space is

> the sum total of homogeneous objects (phenomena, states, functions, figures, variable meanings, and so on), between which relations exist which

are similar to normal spatial relations (continuity, distance, and so on). In viewing a given sum of objects as space, we ignore all the properties of these objects except for those which are defined by the spatially similar relations which we are considering. (Lotman 1977, 217–18)[8]

In other words, telling stories is a process of "modeling, and enabling others to model, an emergent constellation of spatially related entities" (Herman 2002, 296). To imagine a setting involves not only visual processes of knowledge but also first and foremost what Bruner as well as the psychologist Victor Nell have called "propositional knowledge." This knowledge concerns making judgments about the space and feeds on the more concrete images that a text may contain. In *Lost in a Book*, Nell illuminates the distinction with the following examples:

> If I am asked whether an elephant is bigger than a mouse, I draw on over-learned propositional information and require no image. However, if I have to say whether a mouse or a hamster is larger, I must generate an image, because propositionally both mouse and hamster belong to the same category, "small." Similarly, there are questions for which the proposition file has no answer at all, such as "Is a horse's knee or the tip of its tail higher off the ground?" If we translate this information back to the reading process, there are clearly narrative frames for which no images are necessary, such as the hero's good-natured face or the flash of his blue eyes. On the other hand, there are descriptions of new and unusual creatures or machines for which the reader must generate an image in order to understand the narrative. (1988, 219)

Converting verbal images into visual impressions and spatial relationships, however, is merely one way to establish a literary space because it is only concerned with the role played in texts by spatial indicators. Of equal importance to the study of chronotopes is the semantic dimension of the narrative space. This second key phenomenon is also based on propositional knowledge, constituting an additional source of schematization of the literary space.

THE ABSTRACT REPRESENTATION OF SPACE
Literary images of space possess a semantic surplus—a symbolic meaning—which Helmut Meyer (1957) refers to as "sinnbezogene Räume" [symbolic spaces]. A literary setting may have a frightening effect or provoke euphoria because we detect connotations of other dangerous or exciting situations in it. The visual element of dark spaces in film noir, for example, evokes a series of associations with mystery, danger, and imminent threat. In addition, a setting is perfectly able to convey the narrative's specific symbolic charge. The castle, in Kafka's novel of that name, is

not just a place situated high on an elevated part of the town; in its spatiality, it also acquires the symbolic meaning of being inaccessible. At this symbolic level, the literary space also proves to be open to reductionism and schematization. As illustrated by Kafka's symbolism of height, these symbolic spaces are remarkable in the sense that they are able to shed entirely the visual link. The images of space referred to in descriptions (at the level of sentences and in the representation of action episodes) mainly allude to visual impressions and spatial relationships, whereas symbolic spaces activate abstract processes of thought. According to Michael Denis, the empirical research of Walter Perrig and Marc Marschark, among others, shows that "during the processing of a narrative, visual imagery contributes highly to the encoding of 'microstructures' (such as sentences), but that it has no direct connection with the processes responsible for thematic storage of text" (1991, 132). Something similar seems to be happening in the construction of symbolic spaces. To describe trees in a forest, for example, is of an entirely different order than to evoke the emotional and cognitive connotations of "una selva oscura." In the latter case (when we are reading the opening sentences of Dante's *Divina Commedia*), our imagination operates at a different, more complex level.

The majority of the chronotopes mentioned by Bakhtin are situated on this level of increased complexity. The chronotope of the medieval chivalric romance is called a "wondrous" space (Bakhtin 1981a, 154). A space of this sort contains hardly any visual referents.[9] More than anything, it is a set of visualizable images (the fight with the dragon at the cave, the encounter with the dwarf in the woods) that becomes the object of evaluations or connotations by way of an additional mental operation. The visual denotata are merely pretexts for a judgment at a secondary stage. These secondary-stage images are special because they are arranged through semantic relationships. The mind is spontaneously inclined, for example, to mark out a strange, perilous world against other images that suggest a more familiar, peaceful world. Thus, the literary space becomes a complex of abstract spaces that are interconnected.[10] Consequently, the secondary, more complex level of narrative imagination equally involves images that arise from propositions. In this case, however, the propositions concern not only the relationships between visual denotata but also the thematic content with which these relationships are charged.

This ability of narratives to give shape to relationships between abstract spaces and processes and assign thematic value to them is exceptionally important for the study of chronotopes. This is because, as an analysis of narrative-coordinating plot developments would be able to demonstrate, another spatiality seems to be at work here. Gabriel Zoran, David Herman, Marie-Laure Ryan, and Zsófia Sztranyiczki correctly observed that "cognitive mapping" also operates at the level of the larger whole, that narrative imagination at the level of the entire "storyworld" leads to a "totalizing, bird's-eye view mental image of narrative space" (Ryan 2003a, 236).

By delimiting the action-spatial stage of imagination from the plot-spatial stage, we can show that the chronotopes of narrative imagination operate in different spheres. In the case of plot-space chronotopes, the spatial indicators are of a general nature. They refer to a complex of spaces that are important to the plot. Thus, the fictional world of an adventure tale often consists of two contrasting spaces: a space for the principal characters to feel at home in and a space in which to live their adventures (the alien world). Research by Vladimir Propp and Joseph Campbell on these kinds of fairytales demonstrates that the plot provides some variation in these spaces: the hero transgresses the frontier with the alien world, solves a few problems, and returns (a richer man) to the familiar world. Knowing that recipients spontaneously interconnect such images of space while reading or watching a story, we can conclude that narrative imagination at this spatial level consists in an Archimedean, totalizing view of the storyworld.

METAPHORICAL FORMS OF SPATIALITY

The spatial effects in narrative imagination can assume even more radical schematic forms. At the tertiary stage of metaphorical abstraction, mental images adopt the form of worldviews, both ethically and metaphysically. In the Neoplatonic metaphysics of Plotinus and Augustine, oppositions, such as high and low, are part of the argument's core: from the higher world, the spirit has to descend into the lower world of matter, or, vice versa, the spirit must attain the higher world through a gradual liberation from the material world. In the politics of modern democracies, the opposition between left and right is fundamental (representing reform or conservation of the existing political, economic, and social systems). In feudal political systems, by contrast, it is the opposition of high and low that constitutes the doxa. In (racial or other) separatist worldviews, the oppositional pairs of near/ remote and inside/outside constitute the interpretational axes for judgments on social cohesion and social upheaval. Finally, the oppositional pair open and closed respectively denotes tolerance and bigotry in an ethical sphere (see Karl Popper's open and closed societies, inspired by Henri Bergson).

Lotman claims cultural models of this sort do not possess any concrete spatial representations but are nonetheless understandable as spatial metaphors. He further avers that "on the level of supra-textual, purely ideational modeling, the language of spatial relations turns out to be one of the basic means for comprehending reality" (Lotman 1977, 218). Lotman is correct to declare that mental images of this kind possess "completely non-spatial content." We will see that over the centuries narrative genres have been subject to influences from worldviews like these. They adapt their plot-spaces to the spatial relationships contained in the worldview. In his study of François Rabelais, Bakhtin mentions the transition from a medieval, vertical worldview dominated by the high-low opposition into a Renaissance representation governed by the horizontal axis of time. According to him, the traces of this transition can be detected in the narrative space of literary texts.[11] The same phenomenon takes place with the transition from a narrative imagination ruled by a Euclidean concept of space to a new strategy of imagination anticipating the Bergsonian view of space (dominated by openness, change, and creativity).

The Unity of Time and Space in Narrative Imagination

In the preceding discussion, I attempted to demonstrate that any realization of time presupposes a spatial context. I have also described the literary space from the perspective of the narrative actions that are performed within it. Nevertheless, I would like to take a closer look at the unity of time and space.

Almost every observer (Morson, Holquist, Tara Collington, Jay Ladin) appears to stress the mutual interaction between time and space, but not everyone takes the analysis to the three levels of imagination I have distinguished in the previous section. Bakhtin, however, seems deeply aware of the complexity and the multiple layers of spatiotemporal interaction. One of his remarks on the issue is found in what is perhaps the most frequently quoted excerpt in chronotope research:

> In the literary artistic chronotope, spatial and temporal indicators are fused into one carefully thought-out, concrete whole. Time, as it were, thickens, takes on flesh, becomes artistically visible; likewise, space becomes charged and responsive to the movements of time, plot and history. The intersection of axes and fusion of indicators characterizes the artistic chronotope. (1981a, 84)

Bakhtin emphasizes the complex nature of narrative imagination in the final part of the second sentence and in the last one. In the clause about space being responsive to "the movements of time, plot and history," he distinguishes three forms of time largely corresponding to my previously mentioned three stages of abstraction. *Time* corresponds with time in its concrete manifestation, in a concrete spatial context. *Plot* resides as a semantic construct at the more abstract level of the fictional world. Finally, Bakhtin mentions the stage of the *worldview*, which is the most abstract and is where the time of history—whether cosmic or human—provides our abstract representations of the world with a pattern. Moreover, Bakhtin states that the indicators of time, plot, and history are interwoven and that the three levels of abstraction ("axes") intersect.[12] Hence, there is a need to elucidate the three types of imagination by means of narratological theories and to demonstrate how the stages and textual indicators in narrative imagination arise from and react to each other.

ACTION-SPACE CHRONOTOPES AS (INTERTEXTUAL) SCRIPTS

Narrators use the chronotopes of imagination as "methods for artistically fixing time and space" (Bakhtin 1981a, 86). Without them, a story would not be a story but a treatise. The most important level of the narrative is the lowest level of imagination. The action-space chronotope, writes Bakhtin,

> serves as the primary point from which "scenes" in a novel unfold, while at the same time other "binding" events, located far from the chronotope, appear as mere dry information and communicated facts. . . . Representation is concentrated and condensed in a few scenes and these scenes cast a light that makes even the "informing" parts of the novel seem more concrete. (1981a, 250)

In a narrative, those scenes that enable relationships on the second level of imagination are important. The chronotopes of equilibrium and conflict, discussed in the next chapter, meet this criterion. They constitute powerful images that are of fundamental importance for narrative imagination.

Equally powerful is the attraction generated by Bakhtin's view of the human imaginative faculty, which largely explains the great success the chronotope concept has had in recent years (see Bemong et al. 2010). This success has unfortunately also spawned a number of misgivings. For example, the chronotope concept is used to develop needlessly complex arguments that only pertain to the setting of a story (Ladin 1999, 214). Some studies in current literary and film theory talk about "urban chronotopes" (Könönen 2003, 14), the "chronotope of film noir" or "the chronotope of the sea" to stress the importance of location to a group of stories. The temporal aspect in these studies quickly degenerates to mere Zeitgeist determining the local color of the setting and the *Sitz im Leben* [situation in life, sociological condition] of the author.

I have already mentioned the importance of space in the recollection of stories; thus, I am well aware of a setting's significance for narrative imagination, but it seems to be more fruitful if we maintain the utmost rigor in connecting spaces with temporal developments and, more specifically, with the actions that take place in the course of these developments.[13] In a psychological study, Amy Coplan observes that "several recent empirical studies indicate that readers tend to adopt a position within the spatiotemporal framework of narratives that is based on the position of the protagonist" (2004, 141). Spaces, in other words, are far from absolute in the reality of imagination. Relative to the action, the movements of the principal character, and other narrative processes such as natural disasters or nonhuman characters, we can observe the creation of relative spaces—as if it were a Gestalt law from the psychology of perception.[14]

The fact that time transforms the narrative space into a relative space is, by the way, also obvious from the art of the *moving image*. Filmmakers perfectly understand that a moving object or a moving character will become the center of attention. Even if the movement progresses toward the side of the frame, the moving object is almost automatically understood to be the central piece of information in the image. A recipient's attention is wholly absorbed by "moving characters." On the contrary, characters who function as obstacles are more quickly perceived as background, a part of the narrative's spatial environment.

It is, therefore, useful for an analysis of imagination to proceed from elementary images that can rightly be called spaces of action. Bakhtin seems to confirm this method when he states that a chronotope serves as a basis for

> the representability of events. And this is so thanks precisely to the special increase in density and concreteness of time markers . . . that occurs within well-delineated spatial areas. It is this that makes it possible to structure a representation of events in the chronotope (around the chronotope). (1981a, 250)

Postformalist narratology has given an initial impetus to the description of narratives on the basis of these types of concrete operations of the imagination. In cognitivist narratology and pragmatic semiotics (basically the forms of narratology that were inspired by C. S. Peirce), some concepts have been developed that seem very inspiring for the study of the building blocks of narrative imagination.

Indeed, it is possible to explain an action-space chronotope by defining it as an image that is summoned on the basis of narrative episodes. The latter are defined by David Herman as a whole of "states, events and actions that involve an identifiable participant or set of participants equipped with certain beliefs about the world and seeking to accomplish goal-directed plans" (2005, 83; 2002, 84).[15] These episodes generate a four-dimensional mental image in the imagination, which combines the three spatial dimensions with the fourth, the structure of the temporal action.

Literary theory has a vast record of studying action-spaces. One of the most interesting exponents of this tradition is Eco. Referring to the concept of "memory schema" from cognitive science (Frederic Bartlett, Teun Van Dijk, Marvin Minsky, Herman), Eco applies the term "script" in his essay *Lector in fabula* to illuminate the imaginal operations I call action-space chronotopes. Indeed, "script" designates a psychological phenomenon not a textual one: scripts are the imagined events that spontaneously emerge when we are reading texts. Whenever the word "woods" occurs, the reader instantly knows the word to be associated with trees, paths, walks, and wolves. Cognitivist psychology has shown these imaginal entities to possess a certain advanced structuring. In our memory, they give shape to a "virtual text or a condensed narrative" (Eco 1989, 106).[16] When a text mentions a girl deep in the woods, we spontaneously call to mind the image of a girl walking down a path between the trees, possibly worrying about a wolf. As such, it is striking to notice the similarity with chronotopes: just as a chronotope does, a script contains a clear development in time (the course of the narrative) and a series of spatial relationships of a schematic nature. In both cases, summary textual indications (the mentioning of "girl" and "woods") suffice to bring about a series of structured operations of thought in the recipient's brain. If a narrative element calls forth associations with a component of a certain memory scheme, the recipient will automatically dig up the whole script (chronotope) from his memory. Even if a script's events are not explicitly mentioned in the narrative component, the recipient can—for instance, on the basis of a spatial setting's representation—still proceed to call to mind the entire "condensed story." When, for example, a person reading a western story imagines a gun fight, he or she partially appeals to a condensed story retrieved from his or her memory, which probably ended up there after watching a film or television show.

The most interesting aspect of the similarity between action-space chronotopes and scripts or memory schemes resides in the possibility to connect chronotopes with literary theory concepts such as intertextuality. As is commonly known, Bakhtin is one of the pioneers of the intertextuality concept (see Julia Kristeva). The study of intertextuality, however, has seen an evolution toward newer concepts, such as "possible worlds," "script," and "scenario." Bakhtin has gradually disappeared out of sight during this evolution. By way of the chronotope concept, both theoretical traditions can be reunited again with the purpose of establishing a productive fusion of methodologies (see also Keunen 2000b).

Eco correctly states that the most relevant scripts in the reception of narratives presuppose a specific cultural specialization or "prior literary knowledge" (1989, 110). For this reason, he calls those scripts that are of greatest interest to the analysis of the imaginal world "intertextual scripts." These are stereotyped formulas of imagination that are dug up from memory while we are reading texts (but also while we are watching films) and enter into a relationship with the narrative. Thus, a specific literacy needs to be present. A person needs to be familiar with a repertoire of imaginal formulas. Someone who never reads detective stories and never watches any private-eye films will only to a limited extent be capable of associating the intertextual script of "big city blues" with a person walking or contemplating the empty, dark streets of a city that glimmer with neon light. Only the trained recipient of this particular culture will see the image of "the loner in the city" as adumbrating imminent doom or representing the lonesome fight of the individual against the urban underworld.

The ability to call up intertextual scripts, in other words, involves the ability to establish intertextual relationships between elements of a specific narrative repertoire or genre. Fixed formulas as well as fixed schemas of action situations and processes are stored in the memory of narrators and their public. In his analysis of these "intertextual scripts," Eco amply demonstrates the way in which audiences and narrators activate these kinds of formulas during the reception or creation of stories.[17] He distinguishes four types of formulas: maximal scripts, motivational scripts, situational scripts, and rhetorical scripts. The first type is an imaginal formula that covers the entire course of a narrative and consequently falls outside of the scope of the study of action-space chronotopes. The three other forms of intertextuality, however, perfectly illuminate the concept.

In a rhetorical script, the image consists of a type of action and a stereotyped setting. A fine example of this is the clichéd depiction of a love scene in the medieval *locus amoenus* (Eco 1989, 109). The image summoned by a *locus amoenus* is composed of a patch of grass, a tree, a small stream of water, and a couple in love. Other examples are the images of horsemen riding through a desert landscape (indicating that the action will follow the conventions of the western) or the creepy keep of a gothic novel.

Situational scripts are imaginal formulas that consist of spatially situated characters and objects (landscapes as well as isolated objects) on the one hand and series of action sequences on the other. Such a script constitutes a more complex intertextual image because the action that is described is not just any type of action. On the contrary, the script focuses on one particular action. This is the case with images from a western staging a shoot-out between good and evil characters in a small town of the Wild West. Other examples are found in the silly fumbling of the dumb attendant or in the femme fatale's seduction attempts. It should be noted that these images strongly resemble the functions gathered by Propp in his *Morphology of the Folktale* (1928). It is no coincidence that images featuring key moments of plot development enjoy a strong intertextual diffusion. Because narratives thrive on moments of conflict, it is exactly those passages, where the antagonist and assisting characters are introduced or commanding characters are described, that make a lasting impression. This is also the reason why these passages lend themselves very well to intertextual transfer.

Situational scripts are deployed to put the completion of a part of the narrative on the right track. As a result, they can vary according to the position they hold in the course of action. A duel, for example, can seal the hero's victory as well as represent a stage of his (temporary) demise. This is not the case with motivational scripts, which involve a series of action-spaces that follow each other closely. They concern, in other words, a tightly joined series of situational or rhetorical scripts. In addition, Eco sees these motivational scripts to be connected with a stereotyped mood. Consequently, this third type of imaginal formula must be considered as a more abstract form of imagination.

As I have already shown, emotional or cognitive connotations indicate a space that is being judged as a whole. This is also apparent from Eco's example of the image of the damsel in distress. This type of script originates from horror literature. It produces (at least) two characters, a chase, and a dark castle, and represents the thematic core of the narrative. This, after all, is just the way horror stories go: helpless heroes end up in crisis situations (as a rule a labyrinthine space with multiple obstacles) because of a villain's actions. Intertextual scripts of this type, in other words, are responsible for disseminating large portions of stories, thus rapidly giving the impression that the recipient is dealing with a stereotyped story or a genre film. Ridley Scott's science fiction horror film *Alien* (1979), for example, appeals to numerous stereotypes of the science fiction genre while at the same time maintaining the essence of the chase script that flourished in the gothic novel.

THE INTERACTION OF ACTION-SPACE AND PLOT-SPACE CHRONOTOPES

It appears from the above-mentioned definition of motivational script that action-spaces are, in some cases, a bridge toward plot-spaces. They provide unity between different action-spaces (for example, situational and rhetorical scripts). It is mainly—but not exclusively—these imaginal formulas Bakhtin has in mind when he calls chronotopes the "organizing centers" of the narrative and claims that these imaginal entities are the place "where the knots of narrative are tied and untied" (1981a, 250).

To investigate the components of narrative imagination in a particular story, not *all* chronotopes need to be analyzed. It suffices to extract those episodes in which the recipient's imagination is exceptionally stimulated. The same applies when this is considered from the narrator's perspective: the creator of an imaginal construct, the author or filmmaker, selects key passages from the narrative course he or she has in mind and tries to highlight these in such a way that they will direct the recipient's imagination.[18] Action-spaces in specific key passages function not only as anchor points in order to understand other events but also as tools to enable thematic unities (even as far as the resulting plot development) or emotional qualifications (including the admiration for or aversion to a literary work). In short, action-spaces function as tools that help us construct an image of the plot-space in its totality.[19]

The description of plot-spaces is a tricky endeavor. It only seems to be possible for stereotyped narratives (like fairytales) and paraliterature. Eco even distinguishes a separate intertextual script for the latter form of literature, which he calls the "maximal script." Paraliterary texts (as well as some forms of trivial literature, such as the romance novel or crime stories of the whodunit-type) use stereotyped storylines that could be called prefab-fabulas. All (or nearly all) characters receive a stereotyped interpretation, and the narrative progress is also stereotyped: stereotyped evolution in time, stereotyped heroes, and a stereotyped spatial setting (Modledski 1982, Radway 1984). Only the spatial details (names, color of hair, location) and temporal details (repetition of one or the other action sequence) seem to vary. The fact that Mills and Boon provided their writers with computer schemas that merely needed "completion" proves that the imaginal formulas in this case were comprehensive and nearly totalitarian. However, it is not impossible to conceive of an implicitly maximal script for the more creative kinds of narrative as well. Indeed, it is frequently possible to distinguish imaginal constructs that visualize and "map" the totality of a narrative on the basis of what Eco calls motivational scripts, in which the time of the plot fuses with a spatial representation and thus becomes plot-space.

Through much of the life of theory, plot-spaces had never been discussed in narratology. In 2003, however, Ryan introduced the idea of a "map of the plot" in "Narrative Cartography: Toward a Visual Narratology." With regard to plot-cartography, readers undertake attempts to reassemble logical relationships between the events in the lives of characters into one whole. They make attempts at synthesizing the interactions that occur during the course of life, and they try to picture for themselves the global increase of tension (Ryan 2003b). Action-spaces should not be conceived "like the pieces of a puzzle, for this would mean that comprehensive images of textual space cannot be fully formed before the end of the text." They instead constitute elements that are situated into a more abstract spatial schema during the course of the reception process: "readers work from the very beginning with a global, but very schematic, vision of the spatial configuration of the textual world" (Ryan 2003a, 236).

A previous attempt to conceptualize this secondary-level-imagination is found with Lotman. Preceding Ryan by twenty years, he gave the initial impetus to a theory of the "plot-space" in two of his texts. In *The Structure of the Artistic Text*, Lotman writes that a narrative is characterized by its closed nature. He concludes his explanation of a narrative text's "frame" with the observation that the beginning and the end of a text delineate the storyworld's frame:

> In a work of art the course of events comes to a halt when the narrative is broken off. Nothing further takes place, and it is understood that the hero, alive up to that moment, will not die, that the man who has found love will not lose it, that the conqueror will not in the future be conquered, for all further action is precluded. This reveals the dual nature of an artistic model: while reflecting a separate event, it simultaneously reflects a whole picture of the world; in recounting the tragic fate of a heroine, it speaks of the tragic

nature of the world as whole. . . . The structure of the space of a text becomes a model of the structure of the space of the universe, and the internal
syntagmatics of the elements within a text becomes the language of spatial
modeling. (Lotman 1977, 216, 217)

Although Lotman discusses the relation between plot-space (the tragic course of a
narrative) and worldview (the tragic view of life), it also contains a workable definition of the plot-space chronotope. The closed nature of a work, he states, turns
the story into a fenced fictional world, a closed off universe. The cross-cut spaces
reunite in the closed whole as one single image, yet for this image to be called a
chronotope, the actions taking place in the fictional space (the development of
time) must cooperate in determining this image. The example of the tragic heroine
in the above quotation points at this temporal dimension. Even more chronotopic
is the phenomenon Lotman describes in a later text and which applies to the
plot-space of elementary stories. In "The Origin of Plot in the Light of Typology," he states that plot-space and character mutually determine each other. In
simple adventure stories (for example, Propp's adventure tales), heroes are always
the characters who freely move through literary space; heroes are mobile characters "who enjoy freedom with regard to plot space, who can change their place
in the structure of the artistic world" (Lotman 1979, 168). Character and setting,
in other words, become one in the plot-space. Through this unity, a chronotope in
the strict sense of the word arises in the imagination: the space is clearly charged
with development, with process, with movement. Thus, the nonmoving becomes
secondary in the recipient's imagination, a part of the chronotope's element of
setting. Secondary characters—"those who are immobile, who represent, in fact,
a function of this space" (Lotman 1979, 168)—are no longer essential for the
plot-space's image of time because they solely serve the development of time that
propels the principal character.

The imaginal representation of a plot-space is a combination of an integral
narrative-coordinating structure (space) and a sequence of actions performed by
a character (time). This is demonstrated by the manner in which the different
action-spaces are mutually implicated in a narrative. An example may explain this.
In the whodunit, the narrator composes his story by means of successive episodes
in which time after time a new change is revealed. It may not always be useful to
remember all of the changes in order to appropriately interpret the story. The
recipient usually abstracts these changes into a series of three main movements.
Peter Nusser maps these movements as follows. First, the story introduces an antagonist, in the shape of a character committing an enigmatic crime (usually a murder). At least one episode (but often several) is dedicated to this. In the course of
this introduction, the object of the story is presented since the crime is a truth that
remains hidden but must be uncovered in the remainder of the story. Second, the

story will offer a description of the way in which the perpetrator must be tracked down. A detective produces a number of suspects who gather around him. He investigates their alibis and tries to come up with evidence for excluding them one by one. He finds help in clues (not only physical clues but also statements by the suspects) that he gathers here and there but is also obstructed by false clues. In order to elaborate this problem-solving activity, the narrator will dedicate several episodes to all suspects. During this process, the primary suspects are usually considered in a series of connected episodes alternating with episodes focusing on other suspects rather than in order of succession. Moreover, the narrator may insert additional episodes with the purpose of reconstructing (from the clues) the perpetrator's modus operandi and of elucidating his motives. In the third and last movement, the detective unveils the solution and the perpetrator is carried off (Nusser 1980, 26).

Nusser represents the crime story as a linear series of succeeding action-space chronotopes, but the story can equally be pictured as a circular construction. A posteriori, a classical crime story can be reconstructed following Paul Buchloh's scheme:

> Peaceful state before murder → Murder → False clues, secondary murder, etc.
> → Solution → Arrest of murderer → Peaceful state after arrest. (1978, 14)

It appears that the detective story is pressed between two moments of *stasis* (conditions of regularity determining the imaginal representation of the initial and the final episode). Hence, it describes *de facto* a circular movement: the story opens with an episode that stages the upheaval of everyday life (a murder is committed, the introduction of the antagonist), then focuses on hunting down the perpetrator and finding his motives, and finally closes with a return to the harmonious point of departure.

It is clear from this example that a plot-space is the sum of its parts (the action-spaces), but also more than this. The integral image—the circular movement from harmony to harmony regained—cannot be reduced to the action-spaces because it requires a separate imaginal operation. Brooks's *Reading for the Plot* contains appropriate terms for both imaginal operations. Brooks distinguishes between, on the one hand, the proairetic passages of a story in which a specific action is put forward, and on the other hand, the hermeneutic coherence of a story. By means of the terms proairetic and hermeneutic, which Brooks borrows from Roland Barthes' poststructuralist narratology (1970), it is possible to indicate that stories express two forms of temporality. Plot, he states,

> might best be thought of as an "overcoding" of the proairetic by the hermeneutic, the latter structuring the discrete elements of the former into larger

interpretive wholes, working out their play of meaning and significance. (Brooks 1984, 18)

The action-spaces to be decoded with proairetic codes constitute the elements of a lower level of imagination. On a higher level, the recipient visualizes the story-world from a distance. This operation preferably takes place after the closing of the story, but the Archimedean view is already tested during reading, thus giving rise to an anticipating plot-space. Brooks concludes: "Perhaps we would do best to speak of the anticipation of retrospection as our chief tool in making sense of narrative, the master trope of its strange logic" (Brooks 1984, 23).[20]

The problem with Brooks's view of plot-space is that he barely takes into account the spatial embedment of plot and episodes. In order for the proairetic and the hermeneutic, the action-space and the plot-space to "think together," Darko Suvin's (essentially similar) definition seems more appropriate. A narrative, he states, is a

finite and coherent sequence of actions, located in an overarching chrono-tope, and proceeding from an initial to a final state of affairs. Its minimal requirements would be an agent, an initial state changing to a commensurate final state, and a series of changes consubstantial to varying chronotopes. (Suvin 1985, 35)

This definition contains the key elements that were previously discussed. A plot-space is the overarching image that can be represented as a world-in-motion by the characters' actions. Apart from being a temporal given, it is also a spatial given: the actions can be located in the overarching chronotope. Between the initial and final moments of plot development, we find a series of chronotopes that can be called action-spaces and are coherently joined together. These chronotopes continuously interpenetrate each other but do not affect each other in their constructional features; they remain autonomous imaginal constructions. In a passage that may seem enigmatic at first sight, Bakhtin beautifully synthesizes the interaction between both stages of imagination and between the different chronotopes at the lowest stage:

The relationships themselves that exist *among* chronotopes cannot enter into any of the relationships contained *within* chronotopes. The general characteristic of these interactions is that they are *dialogical* (in the broadest sense of the word). But this dialogue cannot enter into the world represented in the work, nor into any of the chronotopes represented in it: it is outside the world represented, although not outside the work as a whole. (1981a, 252; Bakhtin's italics)

The dialogical relationships between action-spaces, Bakhtin emphasizes, constitute relationships between autonomous spatiotemporal constructions. Besides telling their own separate story, autonomous action-spaces also enter into a dialogue with each other through their interaction with the plot-space. On the level of the plot-space, a secondary story arises that neither affects the visualizable action-spaces as such ("the world represented in the work") nor positions itself outside the work of art. It is, in other words, an image at a higher and more abstract stage of the imagination.

TIME AND SPACE IN WORLDVIEWS AND GENRES

Readers of Bakhtin's work have reason to complain about the careless way the concept of chronotope is defined. The explanation for this resides not in Bakhtin's alleged inability to create order in his theory but in the exceptionally complex interactions between the different levels to which the concept of chronotope can be applied. Action-space, plot-space, and worldview are three forms of imaginal constructs that are closely interconnected in practice. Following Bakhtin, plot-space chronotopes can be considered as the core of genres. Yet Bakhtin also teaches that some action-space chronotopes are so genre-specific that the genre can be defined by means of this particular action-space chronotope alone. This is the case, for example, with the labyrinthine architecture in the gothic novel.

It is apparently difficult for genre studies to distinguish between two levels of imagination. Something similar happens when the influence of worldviews, of philosophical views on time and space, is analyzed. Plot-spaces are abstract images that correspond to a fictional world, yet these images are not merely the sum of the action-spaces in this fictional world. The way in which we structure our imagination is largely the same as our manner of structuring the world around us. Consequently, the imagination of a plot-space is indeed very sensitive to influences from worldviews. To add to the confusion, Bakhtin frequently considers worldviews as the basis for typical action-spaces. In this way, the worldview of modernity, for example, influences the threshold chronotope.

In order to adequately describe the complexity of the interactions between the levels of imagination, I must first define the most abstract imaginal constructs—the worldviews—in a more precise way. I must also clearly ascertain whether or not Bakhtin ascribes a very strict meaning to these images. It should be noted that Bakhtin implicitly uses genre concepts as mediators between worldviews and plot-spaces. In his study of chronotopes, he implies that if we want to carry out a profound analysis of the relationship between a worldview and a plot-space, then we simply need to conceive the worldview under consideration as a series of genre conventions because only then will we be able to show that these genre conventions are also present in the storyworld, in the imaginal construct I call the plot-space. The question is, what are the criteria that can be applied to detect these sorts of genre conventions? The answer is in keeping with the previous paragraphs: time and space are the criteria that provide structure to worldviews as well as to plot-spaces.

Action-Space, Plot-Space, and Worldview

In his groundbreaking study of the bildungsroman, Franco Moretti defines the relationship between plot-space and worldview by stating that "plot differences are the most apt to grasp the rhetorical and ideological essence of a historically narrative culture" (Moretti 1987, 7). This view strongly resembles the one formulated by Bakhtin in his study of chronotopes. Bakhtin notes, for example, that the plot-space in classical antiquity was a very artificial and static construction with hardly any opportunity for heroes to change. The Renaissance plot, by contrast, was to a great extent attuned to the changeability of the hero. In "Epic and Novel," a text from the same period, Bakhtin stresses the closed nature of the epic, associating it with a mythical worldview. The novel, however, is linked to the individualism and open social structure of bourgeois modernity. In other words, Bakhtin connects the secondary-level-imagination (the integral fictional world) with the imaginal strategies existing outside the narrative.

It is striking to note that he thinks of the latter worldviews as spatial-temporal constructions. Against the backdrop of antiquity's static worldviews, Bakhtin sees a preference for a stable space, where change is of subordinate importance and time moves in a cyclical fashion, and explicitly refers to the philosophy of time I will later call *idealistic eschatology*. In turn, the worldview corresponding to the novel's plot-space is an immanent space characterized by everyday contingencies where time exhibits a linear pattern (corresponding to *realistic eschatology*).

Bakhtin's preference for worldviews is at its strongest in the manuscript about the bildungsroman (which was also written in the 1930s). In his opinion, the traditional adventure novel displays the same pattern: the heroes deploy their activities in a static world (time and space obey the rules of building up tension), and as a consequence of this world model, they are not able to develop their identities. Illustrations of this can be found in the satirical novels written in the fashion of Apuleius or Petronius and in the adventure novel, with its variants of the chivalric epic romance, the adventure-filled saints' lives, or the Baroque adventure novel— all of these are genres that I will rename as regeneration and mission chronotopes. Bakhtin also observes a clear connection between the world model and the nature of novelistic action in the bildungsroman of the late eighteenth century. This type of novel will prove to be fundamental for all later types of a realistic narrative art. In it, the hero becomes a dynamic character by being situated in a social world charged with historical dynamics. These examples show that for Bakhtin a worldview does not represent a content view of the world but an abstract pattern, a cognitive tool. Recent narratological studies corroborate this hypothesis:

Causality not only manifests itself in connections among the events of the story but also is a key aspect of the storyworld represented via narrative texts. Every fictional universe has distinctive ontological features (see Ryan 1991, 31–47) and each operates under a set of causal laws. The system of causation that governs a narrative is as central an element of its setting as are the related components of space and time. (Richardson 2005, 50)

In opposition to Brian Richardson's analysis of four types of storyworlds (supernatural, naturalistic, aleatorical, and metafictional), I would like to attain more qualified distinctions by way of an analysis of the philosophy of time and the worldview. It seems to me that more interesting categories are to be found in views of causality and time insofar as they are bound up with specific historical developments. Very little research in this field exists within narratology. Bakhtin, however, turns out to be a supportive source. In his work, plot-spaces such as "the folkloric chronotope," "the Rabelaisian chronotope," "the idyllic chronotope," and "the chronotope of the Rogue, the Clown, and the Fool" refer to the worldview he defines by means of Renaissance cognitive strategies. For its part, the eschatological worldview returns in plot-spaces as "the chronotope of the adventure novel of ordeal," "the chronotope of the adventure novel of everyday life," "the chronotope of the chivalric romance," or "the chronotope of ancient biography and autobiography."

Bakhtin takes Moretti's view of differences in plot structures one step further: he not only investigates the relationship between plot-space and worldview but also takes a look at the ways in which intertextual scripts (action-space chronotopes) can be infused with cognitive patterns. By doing so, he detects traces of a dynamic view of time and an immanent spatial pattern in the action-spaces of the works of Rabelais.[21] Linking up action-spaces with worldviews turns out to be an interesting path of thought because Bakhtin can thus prove that a text will sometimes contain references to old worldviews that are unwittingly adopted by the author. Action-space chronotopes, Morson and Emerson state, often belong to a literary tradition. By way of the worldviews that shine through in the action-space, they call forth the recollection of that literary tradition. Morson and Emerson call this phenomenon "genre memory" and define it as follows:

A particular sort of event, or a particular sort of place that usually serves as the locale for such an event, acquires a certain chronotopic aura, which is in fact the "echo of the generic whole" in which the event typically appears. (1990, 374)

A particular action-space chronotope originating from an ancient culture is still able to play a role in a narrative. The Menippean satire plays such a role in Fyodor

Dostoevsky's work, causing his texts to be impregnated by a series of action patterns that recall an alternative way of conceiving worlds.

From concepts such as genre memory, it becomes clear that even when Bakhtin seems to analyze concrete textual elements, he actually has something else in mind. Consequently, Holquist stresses:

> At one extreme, chronotope has a relatively restricted set of applications that apply to literary texts conceived as single units. But chronotope may also be used as a means for studying the relation between text and its times, and thus as a fundamental tool for a broader social and historical analysis, within which the literary series would be only one of several interconnected types of discourse. It is at this level that the chronotope's contribution to a historical poetics may best be seen. (1990, 113)

The historical poetics Bakhtin intended to construct, or so the subtitle of the study of chronotopes suggests, is foremost a study of the historical development of narrative imagination. He attempts to find patterns in texts and to point out how these patterns fall back on cognitive models that are also used outside of literature. Bakhtin, in other words, reads texts from the perspective of genre theory.

Plot-Space and Genre Conventions

In a sense, genres are synonymous with worldviews in Bakhtin's work. He emphasizes that genre classes function as paradigms giving shape to the world. They are imaginal matrices that apply selections to possible literary material and transform it into a fictional world. In fact, the matrices of genre used in everyday life (the genres Bakhtin calls "primary genres") play a similar paradigmatic role. Love letters are never read in the same way as a journalistic report because the world constructed in both genres displays different features. The world of the love letter bases itself on recollected locations, important moments or features of the relationship (a person's power of attraction, emotional effects on the other person, etc.), whereas a report refers to phenomena gathered by empirical observation.

Analogous to such genres, Bakhtin delineates textual classes within literature that individually fulfill paradigmatic roles. He calls these genres "secondary genres." In *The Formal Method* (Medvedev and Bakhtin 1928), secondary genres (that is, classes of literary texts) are understood as strategies of conceiving the world:

> Every significant genre is a complex system of means and methods for the conscious control of reality. . . . Human consciousness possesses a series of inner genres for seeing and conceptualizing reality. . . . The artist must learn to see reality with the eyes of the genre. (Medvedev 1978, 133,134)

Narratives, and more specifically the fixed patterns that recur in all individual narratives (genre codes or conventions), constitute matrices of experience. They mold the storyworld after the patterns of a worldview.

By strictly connecting genre conventions with temporal and spatial patterns, Bakhtin renews genre studies, a discipline that lost much of its credit in literary theory's establishment after World War II. The problem with existent genre theories is the bias with which time or space is often emphasized or used in detecting genre conventions. The method used by communication theorists and journalists is certainly biased. Their genre theories proceed from a dominant feature of spatial representations. The invariants that result from this method rely on the "presentation" of a story. Works unfolding in an alien, future space (with all sorts of strange machines and alienating creatures) are called science fiction, whereas stories situated in police environments are called police or detective novels. A western is a genre term referring to the spatial attributes of the Wild West (desert, horses, Native Americans). We can merely open our television program guides to see that in most cases inventories are made by offering little more than a description of the sorts of spaces in which the actions take place.

In addition to this, some theories of genre have placed the deciding factor squarely in the temporal dimension of narratives. Stories are arranged in groups on the basis of their order of time or plot structure. Well-known examples of temporally focused genre theories are those of Northrop Frye and Ronald Crane. They focus on the type of hero present in a narrative culture, which forms the basis for distinguishing possible plot developments in which the hero can partake.

Crane singles out three types of plot: the "plot of action," in which the hero's situation changes in the course of the story; the "plot of character," in which the hero's moral condition is transformed; and the "plot of thought," in which change is located at the level of the most personal views and emotional attitudes. Frye bases his successful classification theory for Western narrative culture on the Aristotelian typology of heroes. He subsequently connects this with the plot schemes of the tragic and the comic designed by Gustav Freytag: respectively, the plot development leading to the hero's isolation and a scheme of the hero ultimately opting for integration in some larger whole. Following the Aristotelian classification in superior, equal, and inferior characters, Frye describes the evolution of narrative culture as a development in five stages. Each stage introduces a new way of storytelling by propagating a new way of identification and five particular types of narrative culture. A mythical narrative culture characterizes its protagonists as superior to everything and everybody; the characters are gods who exist entirely separate from empirical reality and from the ordinary mortals populating this reality (Frye 1973, 33). A heroic narrative culture (Frye uses the term "romantic," from romance or heroic stories) employs heroes and heroines who are also superior to everything and everyone but nonetheless obey the laws of the finite, transient world. They are of mortal and not divine caliber. Above the empirical world, they live in a realm that can be called fantastic (including fairies, etc.) and is associated in our minds with legends and fairytales. These heroes and heroines are equally found in an epic narrative culture, the third type. In this case, however, the heroes and heroines merely stay in our world—a world that can also judge and rebuke them, or confront them with the forces of nature. This is the culture described in the epics and tragedies of Greek antiquity, which were still in circulation in the Renaissance and the Baroque (Mori 1997). Each of the three aforementioned narrative cultures is concerned with the ruling elite facing a crisis. The fourth type of narrative culture is described by Frye as literature having a "mimetic" concept of the storyworld. It does not concern high mimesis (the "sublime realism" typical for the third type) and instead focuses on the low mimesis of everyday characters. The narrative culture in which these figures thrive best is that of the modern novel. From the Renaissance onward, bourgeois characters will inhabit the storyworlds. Additionally, they are also found in comic plays. To conclude, the fifth type of narrative culture is populated by the most inferior and *pitiful* heroes and heroines, emerging numerously in late modern culture. The characters of twentieth-century literature, for example, belong to the culture of estrangement in which narrators and recipients look down on the frustration and absurd fate of small individuals.

Frye and Crane constructed fairly general theories, which were subsequently completed by the detailed analyses of a handful of other theorists. Building on the tripartite classification of Crane, Norman Friedman, one of his pupils, develops fourteen categories. He introduces distinctions in the plot of action, the plot of character, and the plot of thought. He does this by way of variations in characters (sometimes sympathetic, sometimes vicious; sometimes strong, sometimes weak) and variations on the reactions that the combination of their character traits and fates evoke in the audience. In this way, "the pathetic plot" (typified by a wretched weak character) is identified as a subdivision of the action plot (Friedman's "plots of fortune"). "The education plot" (the protagonist learns something important) is identified as a subcategory of the idea plot (Friedman's "plots of thought").[22] Another variant of Crane's method is found in Christopher Booker's *The Seven Basic Plots*, which identifies plots including "overcoming the monster" and "rags to riches."[23]

The merit of these studies is certainly great. We could even be inclined to call them heroic in their penchant for completeness. Nevertheless, there has been no actual progress in narrative imagination research emanating from these sorts of studies. To do nothing more than detect thematic clusters in narrative time patterns is not sufficient. Our first concern should be to explain the reason *why* such images are relevant. If we fail to show which cognitive strategies lie behind narrative images, then we will create little more than an inventory of literary images.

There is no need to fall back on a storyworld's thematic elements (such as the spatial presentation or the hero or heroine's course of life) in order to categorize narratives within genre groups. Indeed, the reverse is needed; we need to study the ways of structuring a narrative and to connect these with the prevailing types of thought outside of narrative imagination. Only when plot-spaces are connected with worldviews can genres become efficient research categories. In the following section I will attempt to demonstrate that action-spaces are infused with culturally determined views and that plot-spaces show the same congruence to cultural patterns of thought (often through the action-space chronotopes).

2

Concepts of Time and Chronotopes

The method of distinguishing between levels of abstraction (action-space, plot-space, and worldview) clearly establishes the fact that chronotopic constructs can be very different from each other. Sometimes we are dealing with visualizable spaces in which changes take place; sometimes it involves a conglomerate of these spaces synthesized in an abstract image. Worldviews, for their part, are practically stripped of concrete spatial indications.

By making this kind of differential survey of chronotopes, I am, in fact, giving shape to what could be called "the syntax of narrative imagination." Within each syntactical group—on the paradigmatic axis of narrative imagination—numerous alternatives are possible. Depending on the cultural surroundings of the narrative, there is indeed a wide range of actions, plots, and worlds. One of Bakhtin's basic ideas is the hypothesis that these deviations can be explained by studying the differences in concepts of time (1981a, 86). Temporal patterns in plot-spaces, for instance, heavily influence the sort of actions that dominate action-space chronotopes. The example of the whodunit clearly indicates that the temporal pattern is aimed at achieving a goal. A teleological, goal-oriented plot renders some actions possible, or even makes them necessary, thanks to its inherent temporal pattern. Even more important is the influence emanating from the highest level of abstraction. As I will explain in the present chapter, the views of time that characterize a certain worldview influence to a great extent the nature of the plot-space and the outlook of action-spaces.[1]

In his study of chronotopes, Bakhtin implicitly describes the specific ways in which this influence functions. His analysis of the role of concepts of time in action-space chronotopes is twofold, delineating both the influence of the worldview's concept of time and that of the plot-space's concept of time. Equilibrium and conflict chronotopes are initially influenced by more general concepts of time. The basis for these chronotopes is found in the respective temporal concepts of "repetition" and "difference." Because certain narrative images put recurring processes at the center of attention, they are thematically arranged with experiences of equilibrium. Other narrative images, passing through experiences of chance, subsume a position within the range of difference and conflict. Things become more complicated when it comes to determining the influence of the plot-space on action-spaces. Action-space chronotopes numerously occur in the majority of our stories. In addition to this, they are "mutually inclusive, they co-exist, they may be interwoven with, replace or oppose one another, contradict one another or find themselves in even more complex interrelationships" (Bakhtin 1981a, 252).[2]

Readers who possess some insight into narrative structures know that when we are reading, watching, or listening to a story, an immense number of images is "fired" at us. As a result, it is not always clear to us which images are the most significant to the narrator. To make things worse, these images can act in such an autonomous way that we lose ourselves in details. The real art of interpreting a text lies in the singling out of those motifs and images that enable us to discern the narrator's story. Some images in the imaginal world have a propensity of dominating others: "it is common," says Bakhtin, "for one of these chronotopes to envelop or dominate the others" (1981a, 252). In this respect, those episodes and action-spaces that "stick" or "linger on" are most important, which is often confirmed by what we find ourselves saying when we exit a film theater. Of course, not all images succeed in making a lasting impression. Only those images possessing a strong thematic value, images that also produce an effect on the level of the plot-space, can claim a place in the category of dominant chronotopes. As demonstrated above, motif-oriented scripts, for example, are often the right tools for leading a story along the right lines. Because of this, they can function as dominant chronotopes. Chases are crucial in horror stories as events capable of representing the central objective: to get out of a crisis situation. As such, it can be argued that the temporal pattern of a higher level (the goal-oriented aspect or intentionality of the plot) influences the chronotopes on a lower level (that of concrete events).

The chronotopes of equilibrium and conflict that I will highlight in the first section of this chapter belong to the category of dominant chronotopes. These are images of exceptional importance to the temporal pattern of narratives because we are examining images of equilibrium that are often encountered in opening or closing scenes (such as an idyllic opening passage, a happy or tragic ending) and that allude to a state of psychological balance. Furthermore, conflict chronotopes—such as the chase in the gothic novel or moments of psychological crisis in other narratives—are crucial because they generate the fundamental conflicts that provide structure and tension in a narrative.

The image a person calls to mind when scanning the overarching plot logic and the integral fictional world is influenced by the world outside the text. I will distinguish two groups of plot-space chronotopes: teleological and dialogical. This distinction is related to the fact that teleological and dialogical constructs of imagination are closely associated with the concepts of time of two different worldviews. A plot-space that strongly accentuates the closing moment (the eschaton) traces back to judgments about a harmonious universe, whereas a plot-space chronotope accentuating the deciding moments and crises of the characters (the kairos) expresses the basic experience of an unstable universe inhabited by more or less free individuals. Chapter 3 will show that there are numerous possible variations on these two philosophical types. In the second section of chapter 2, "Interaction Between Equilibrium and Conflict: Eschaton and Kairos," I examine the experiential foundations shared by these plot types.

The Action-Space as Equilibrium and Conflict

AION AND TYCHE

Repetition and difference are essential categories of experience. When a phenomenon repeats itself, we can designate this pattern, explain its past, and make predictions. Repetition brings regularity and certainty to the world. By contrast, when a phenomenon deviates from and is unable to be reduced to a pattern, we speak of chance: the event befalls us and ruptures our pattern of expectations. Difference indeed brings turmoil and uncertainty or contingency to the world. The Greeks had separate gods for these two experiential categories: Aion,[3] a time god, ruled the seasons and all other forms of regularity; human beings called upon him in those times that they longed for the eternal repetition. Tyche, the goddess of fortune, chance, providence, and fate (Roman: Fortuna), of the lucky or unlucky star under which mortals are born, represents the unrest people experience in situations that manifestly are beyond their control (see also Köhler 1973, 27).

The two divinities are perfect as expressions of a Western cosmological view that actually sets us apart from other cultures. For example, in shamanist cultures nothing happens by accident or chance. All events are interpreted to be the work of spiritual forces. In Western narrative art, both experiential categories, time and fate, subtly counterbalance each other: sometimes stories call forth predictable and universal situations, and sometimes they allude to unexpected and contingent situations. It is truly impossible to make generalizing statements about the proportional occurrence of the two situations, yet it is quite evident that both categories of experience form an absolute requirement for telling interesting stories. The audience's preference for states of equilibrium clearly stems from a more general, collectively and quasi-unconsciously understood psychological appreciation of order and regularity. At the same time, however, any depiction of the familiar and the unpredictable notably implies a sense of unrest and chaos.

Tyche's contingencies are absolutely vital to the storyteller because stories are only interesting inasmuch as they contain conflicts. Honoré de Balzac once said, "Chance is the greatest novelist of the world; to be productive, we only have to study it." David Herman says something similar in narratological terms when he argues that stories without conflicts inevitably score very low on "tellability" (or "noteworthiness") (2002, 84). Of essential importance to a "tellable" story is "the thwarting of intended actions by *unplanned* events, which may or may not be the effect of other characters' intended actions" (Herman 2005, 83; my italics). Interesting stories show how events elude the expectations and the plans of individuals. In this respect, the archetypes of our narratives are ancient narrative forms like *anecdotes* and *legends*. Anecdotes play an important role in everyday communication: people are frequently caught up in them or cannot stop telling them, whether they are true or made up, serious or funny. Legends are fictional assimilations of anecdotes—think of the popular legends about witches and goat riders that have served as a kind of pseudo-historiography of certain regions for centuries. In both cases, the narrator's focus of attention is on the deviations from the norm.

In novels, too, the most interesting elements consist in anomalies, deviations, or variations. Obviously, they appeal more to the imagination than phenomena that repeat themselves over and over again and, as a result, too closely resemble each other. In the beginning of *Anna Karenina*, Leo Tolstoy rightfully says, "All happy families resemble one another, but each unhappy family is unhappy in its own way." In other words, unrest and contingency are more interesting to work with than regularity and repetition.[4]

An anomaly or deviation may spark interest, yet a story can quickly lose all attraction if it has no point or "pay-off," if it holds no message for the recipient, or if it never asks questions that mean something to the recipient. This is the reason why stories must express values. We need to be able to associate concepts with stories that relate to situations of which we can aesthetically or ethically approve or disapprove. If we are unable to make more or less general valuations, the story becomes boring, as is the case with certain experimental texts like those we use to call the *nouveau roman* (however valuable for other reasons). Whether or not images will stick depends to a large extent on the presence of values. They are mostly found in (images of) situations that confirm the regularity of the world. The archetypal forms of these situations reside in *myths* and *hymns*. Myths form the paragon of narratives in which irregularities are more of an exception and regularity constitutes the rule. The myth applies a concept of time that is actually timeless: the timelessness of eternal truths. Time only matters as the repetition of the same, which is almost the opposite of motion, since a world-in-motion requires differences in moments of time.[5] Lotman (implicitly referring to Bakhtin) says that myths

> reduce the world of anomalies and surprises which surrounds humanity to norm and orderliness. They tell not of one-off exceptional events, but of events which are out of time, endlessly repeated, and in this sense, unchangeable. (1990, 152)

The staging of regularity is also at the heart of (national) hymns or anthems, referring to the harmonious unity of people, nature, and history. These narrative forms are stripped of every tension to make room for an evocation of perfect harmony.[6] Mythical elements, however, can also be found in certain narratives entertaining far lesser ambitions. It is remarkable to see how myths reserve a highly significant position for exactly those situations in which regularity represents the norm and particularly valuable objects or persons are present.[7] It is striking that many popular narratives end with a harmonious situation that achieves a basic human object: a congenial natural environment (the sun setting over a peaceful landscape, a lazy summer day), an euphoric sense of community (the waffle feast in the Flemish comic strip *Nero*, the wild boar banquet in the French comic *Asterix*), or a joyous entrance to a social institution indirectly referring to community life (the princess's marriage, the Hollywood kiss, the trial that serves justice, an ascension to the throne, a public tribute as in *Star Wars* or in pirate movies like *The Sea Hawk*). In addition to this, popular narratives frequently start with a harmonious opening situation that refers either to an essentially collective activity (the presentation of the Gaulish village in *Asterix*, the happiness of an imminent marriage in Greek romances, the 1950s small-town sense of community in Stephen King stories or David Lynch movies) or to a symbiotic unity between the collective life of human beings and the natural or cultural context (the paradise resort of holidays, a day in springtime, the initial peace in the private eye's office).

These images are closely related to the imaginal constructs Bakhtin denotes by the term of "idyllic chronotope." Idylls frequently are hymns of life. The intertextual script of idylls is shared by many types of text. Apart from the classic idylls (Longus's *Daphnis and Chloe* or bucolic poetry with a great fondness for the *locus amoenus*, the idealized place of comfort and safety), it appears not only in sixteenth-century family sagas and sixteenth-, nineteenth-, and twentieth-century pastoral novels, but also in the English sentimental novel, the German bildungsroman, and the Hollywood romantic comedy. Idylls are narrative forms that have an overdeveloped desire to stage regularity and repetition. They thematically favor cyclical processes (repetition of natural phenomena, repetition in social life) occurring in a peaceful space that excludes all possible dangers. In marked contrast with conflict chronotopes, idylls are the antithesis of anecdotes and exciting actions.

In summary, the two poles of Western experiential philosophy are *repetition* or *regularity* on the one hand and *difference* or *chance* on the other hand. Anecdotes or myths are stories exclusively aimed at one experiential pole. Following Lotman, however, I would argue that the majority of our stories is based on a combination of both archetypes:

The modern plot-text is the fruit of the interaction and mutual interference of . . . two polar types of texts (those describing the regular course of events, and those concerned with anecdotal deviation from the course) to influence each other mutually. This interaction largely determined the subsequent fate of the narrative genres. (1990, 153)

A recent definition, building on Lotman's, considers a story to be the interplay of repetition and difference, the interaction between equilibrium and chance: a story is the "disruption of an initial state of equilibrium by an unanticipated and often untoward event or chain of events" (Herman 2005, 83).[8]

It may seem an arbitrary move to make an attempt at arranging narrative imagination according to two concepts of time, yet this categorization has interesting options. By studying the alternation of equilibrium and conflict, a method of establishing genre categories can be devised. Thus, the position occupied by the crucial conflict chronotopes (those that "stick" or "linger on") forms the basis of three groups of genres, which I will present in the next chapter (the chronotopes of mission, regeneration, and degradation). The panorama offered by equilibrium and conflict chronotopes, for their part, is useful in delineating two large groups of plot-spaces. Dialogical plot-spaces operate with psychologized equilibrium and conflict chronotopes and are therefore able to break free from the totalizing teleological conceptions of plot-space.

A TYPOLOGY OF EQUILIBRIUM CHRONOTOPES
Aion and Hestia
A chronotope is called an equilibrium chronotope when it meets two conditions: the space must form a sequestered whole, and the isolated system's temporal pattern must exhibit movements that repeat themselves or at least are repeatable. I have already designated the second condition according to the concept of time associated with the Greek time-god Aion. For the second condition, I would additionally like to introduce the Greek divinity of protection: Hestia, goddess of domestic peace. The marriage of "regularity" and "home" is perfectly brought to the fore in the idyllic chronotope, named after the *eidyllion*, a short, descriptive form of poetry dominated by peaceful rural scenes. The idyll is characterized by a homogenous and isolated space ("the idyllic unity of the place" is preferably found in "a spatial corner," says Bakhtin [1981a, 225]) with a pervasive sense of cyclical time.[9] It highlights the familiarity of mountains, fields, rivers, and homes, and the events that are closely associated with the succession of generations (the cycle of parent-child-grandchild) and natural processes (the cycle of day and night, of seasons, years, and centuries).

The sense of home that comes about in a familiar and cherished environment ("familiar territory" [Bakhtin 1981a, 225]) forms one of the invariants of equilibrium chronotopes. These images are actuated by the desire for hospitable spaces. Complementing these desires is the exclusion of everything inhospitable and unrecognizable. In fairytales (Lüthi 1976), enemies, without exception, live at the edge of the hospitable space or in faraway countries. When the story brings up the alien and the unknown, they are situated in an excluded space: on the other side of the mountains where death and disaster looms; only there can isolation rule and man be irretrievably lost. In the sequestered space of the equilibrium chronotope, all remains "quietly" in place; all elements are neatly described and entered in a mastered, controlled system. This spatial equilibrium is experienced as an "inside" that is supposed to keep out everything that is out of balance.

Michel Foucault would call this a heterotopy, an alternative space that, much like a utopia, is different from the dominant everyday space, yet it is at the same time real and recognizable. An idyllic valley where tourists retreat and a peaceful rural village far away from urban and metropolitan dangers are locations that conceptually approach Foucault's heterotopias: the cemetery, the library, the cruise ship. In "Of Other Spaces," Foucault argues that it is typical for heterotopias to be relative to other spaces. They offer a response to, or constitute a reversal or deviation from, those spaces. Exclusion is the principal feature of images in which idyllic action-spaces are construed, just as it is in the Foucauldian heterotopy.[10] Idyllic images are depictions stripped of everything negative. They cultivate an absolute "inside" and keep the irregular "outside."

The same mechanism of exclusion can be observed in the temporal patterns.[11] Change and temporal development are highly significant in the image of equilibrium. Nonetheless, the balanced action-space is governed by a sense of time that deviates from our everyday notion of temporal development. Time does not move forward in a slow or fast linear way. It is instead a detour from a state of peace and quiet that regains a state of peace and quiet through the medium of actions. Actions in an equilibrium chronotope are conceived in such a way that they wholly confirm the state of equilibrium. When an equilibrium chronotope contains elements of chance and contingency, they will invariably be presented as anomalies or deviations, which additionally benefit the equilibrium. For an idyllic situation of peace and quiet (summertime, the time of fertility) to be able to describe the circle of time, a connection with processes of decay (autumn, culminating in winter's infertility) is a necessary condition. In the same way that fallen leaves form the foundation for new plants to flourish, processes of decay and decline allow for growth. Deviations, in other words, are only indispensable insofar as they occur with one single purpose: to maintain equilibrium in the idyll's closed system.

The social world exhibits a similar cyclical nature: the mature, ripened state is the state of peace and quiet. It is a situation that is pushed and pulled into an ostensible change by processes of decay (aging, death) and processes of growth (regeneration in the form of children, and through the love for the partner who helps bringing the children into the world). In this case, time also continues to operate as an abstract force. The contingencies that occur in ordinary life are canceled out. There is no more room for them in the idyllic story. As a matter of fact, nothing ever changes, nothing unexpected ever happens; only regular changes can become the object of imaginal representation.[12] It is precisely because equilibrium chronotopes are purged from all irregular developments that we spontaneously associate them with happiness, fulfillment, and hope. This further explains why the equilibrium chronotope plays an important part in literary imagination. Frye squarely places the equilibrium chronotope's significance in the fact that it is active as a model for the comic mode, such as in stories that finish happily or celebrate the acceptance of the individual into the greater whole (1973, 43).

In my attempt to define the equilibrium chronotope, and particularly in my analysis of the ways in which abstract spatial metaphors (inside-outside) act as principles of structuration, a hint is given about the influence worldviews exert on the design of action-spaces. Their impact is even more clearly visible in the views of time hiding behind imaginal representations of equilibrium. This is already suggested by the fact that "happiness" is associated with "equilibrium." For that matter every theory that presents religious man as fundamentally accepting the universe asserts to some extent the regularity of time processes. A fine illustration of this can be found in the following words of stoic philosopher Marcus Aurelius, quoted by William James in *The Varieties of Religious Experience*:

> Everything harmonizes with me which is harmonious to thee, O Universe. Nothing for me is too early nor too late, which is in due time for thee. Everything is fruit to me which thy seasons bring, O Nature: from thee are all things, in thee are all things, to thee all things return. (*Meditations*, Book IV, 523; quoted in James 1902)

In summary, regularity is the most substantial feature of religious and metaphysical systems because regularity and repetition emphasize the timelessness of the created and natural world. Every movement essentially constitutes a return to the starting point, an illusion which has very little to do with the notion of time itself. In another text by William James (*A Pluralistic Universe*) we can find a thought, attributed to J. M. E. McTaggart, that represents the simple denial of time (typical of religions) as a consequence of contemplating regularity in absolute terms: "Reality is not in its truest nature a process, but a stable and timeless state" (James 1902).[13]

From Idealistic to Realistic Equilibrium Chronotopes

My typology of the equilibrium chronotope shows that we are dealing with an imaginal construct of a highly idealistic conception. Equilibrium chronotopes concern images that thrive well in the human mind but rarely occur in empirical reality. Because of the fact that they are the result of accentuating the perfect nature of particular processes and situations, these images acquire a certain utopian effect. It is no coincidence that Bakhtin, in seeking a more concrete shape for the historical archetypes of the idyllic, likes to refer to stories about the land of Cockaigne and Greek mythology of the Golden Age (Hesiod).

The described harmonious equilibriums are not of this world; they exist only in the imagination, lack an empirical place, and are literally *ou-topos* (utopia). Utopian constructions produced by the human mind are best subsumed under the heading of philosophical idealism (which, as a matter of principle, puts "idea" before "perception"). It is no coincidence that the architect of philosophical idealism, Plato, uses the concept of Aion to designate the world of forms or ideas (the real world, which in the famous allegory of the cave in *The Republic* is separated from the human world of perception, a shadow world). Following in Plato's tracks, other thinkers conceived theoretical worldviews with greater sophistication engrafted on the mechanisms of the equilibrium chronotope. Consider how Plotinus evaluated time (change, action, movement) in a completely negative way; just as movement is a degradation of quietude, and acting (*praxis*) is a weakened form of contemplation (*theoria*), Plotinus holds "time" to be a corrupt form of eternity. In the temporal (and temporary) order, man focuses on the inferior (the body, the material) and averts himself from the superior or eternal patterns in the universe. For Plotinus, temporal development is the rupture of the equilibrium at the heart of eternity (De Ley 2005). Such a view of the universe is bound to spawn a great many symbols possessing features of the equilibrium chronotope. Augustine used the image of the *civitas Dei*, the City of God, or the Heavenly Jerusalem, to depict the Christian utopia. Applying Plotinus's concept of time, Augustine declares the disharmonious, material world to be of less importance than the experience of Aion that will mark the city of the end of days. Christian texts elaborating on the image of the Heavenly Jerusalem rarely deviate from the Augustinian view. The symbolism is employed with great rigor in epics that recount the fall of cities.

Idealistic equilibrium chronotopes, however, are not the only variants of this type of action-space. A tradition of myths that are related to nature religions runs parallel to the idealistic worldviews. The myths of fertility in James George Frazer's *Golden Bough* (and in T. S. Eliot's recapturing of them in *The Waste Land*) are the best known examples of this alternative tradition. Traces can be found as far back as antiquity: in the bucolic tradition (in which "the idyllic unity of place" functions as "locus for the entire life process" [Bakhtin 1981a, 229]), in Athenian New Comedy, and in the novels of Greek antiquity. In the Roman art of the novel (Apuleius and Petronius), the equilibrium chronotope is never more than a marginal image and rarely central to the development of the story; yet, at the same time, it points at a third type.

In the ancient novel, this fullness of time has a dual character. In the first place, its roots are in a popular and mythological understanding of time's fullness. But these fixed, temporal forms were already in decay. . . . On the other hand, the ancient novel also contained the feeble first efforts at *new* forms for expressing time's fullness—forms related to the uncovering of social contradictions. . . . But these first efforts were too feeble to stave off the collapse of the major epic forms into novelness. (Bakhtin 1981a, 146–47; Bakhtin's italics)

In this quotation, Bakhtin refers to this third type of equilibrium chronotope, equally independent of idealistic worldviews. He calls these kinds of secular or "realistic" equilibrium chronotopes "the ancient complex." Their material consists of empirical processes such as "nature, love, the family and childbearing, death" (Bakhtin 1981a, 230). Concrete elaborations of secular equilibrium chronotopes are found in the oldest forms of the art of the novel (see, for example, the works of Apuleius and Petronius).

Over the centuries, however, the "ancient complex" increasingly came to dominate the limelight, particularly in folkloric traditions and art forms. As a result, its utopian nature was eroded and gradually erased, only to be replaced by allusions to phenomena from the perceptual world. Eventually the secular type no longer tended to the staging of timeless ideals but celebrated the eternal processes in nature and distilled "heterotopias" from it. From the Middle Ages onward and especially in the Renaissance, the time was ripe for a thorough reconceptualization of equilibrium chronotopes. Late medieval images portraying the thief, the scoundrel, and the fool betray a strong inclination to rephrase natural processes (especially bodily functions) with the intent of subsuming them again under the "old matrix."[14] In the Renaissance, Rabelais pioneered the use this material to give a new élan to the art of the romance or novel. From the Renaissance up until the nineteenth century, a strong predilection for idyllic scenes can be observed.

An important part of the art of storytelling is concerned with describing equilibrium chronotopes from an interiorized perspective and with emphasizing the regularity of psychological or mental life—that is, of "happiness."[15] It should be noted that this form of imagination gradually becomes dominant in literature from the eighteenth century onward. Pioneers such as Jean-Jacques Rousseau subject the old folkloric strategies of mimesis to radical change; the folkloric chronotope is sublimated by means of psychologizing strategies. In Rousseau's work, the elements of the folkloric narrative forms function as material "for constituting an isolated individual consciousness" (Bakhtin 1981a, 230). Preromantic writers will continue to create more archaic equilibrium chronotopes (images of popular culture are believed to possess healing and purifying powers[16]), but what essentially matters in their stories is that the equilibrium and other harmonious forms are evoked from an "interior perspective" (Bakhtin 1981a, 231). In the process, the space very frequently loses its "natural" and cyclical nature, yet this loss is sufficiently compensated for by internalized cyclical movement, by accentuated recurring mental processes (such as memory operations).

In this sense, it is fair to say that modern authors continue to hold in high regard the confirmation of values and the creation of circumstances of perfection. The difference, however, is that they now put the experiences associated with these things they value into another context. Pavel's outline of the morphologic evolution in the history of the novel corroborates this assessment: "the eighteenth-century novel, which gave primacy to verisimilitude, asked whether humans are the source of moral law and masters of their own actions" (2006, 3).[17]

A TYPOLOGY OF CONFLICT CHRONOTOPES
Tyche and Hermes

On the one hand, symbolic systems in ancient cultures that accept myths as eternal truths owe much to the highly idealistic equilibrium chronotopes. Folkloric cultures in more recent times, on the other hand, generally forge imaginal entities that bring about a more profane variant of the equilibrium chronotope, thereby undercutting the myth's pervasive action. This hostility of Western narrative culture toward the idealistic myth also manifests itself in another way. In the stories we have been telling ourselves at least since antiquity, human thought, by definition, expresses itself in ambivalent terms about the world. Apart from acknowledging equilibrium chronotopes, these narratives also acknowledge the existence of fundamental conflicts, claiming them to be a necessary part of the structure of the universe.

For Western storytellers, the sublunary world is not merely (and in some cases never) a side effect of the trans- or superlunary world. It also becomes the point of departure for genuine reflection about the external world. The attention given by Western narrative culture to images of conflict proves this point. It could be said that our stories, to some extent, always are anti-utopian and anti-idealistic. Philosophically speaking, the narratives are pluralistic, never absolutist. One of the best formulations of this conflict between idealistic and pluralistic symbolic systems can be found in William James's *A Pluralistic Universe*. The author analyzes the ambivalence that Western man is so keen on talking about as a contrast between two philosophical systems:

The doctrine on which the absolutists lay most stress is the absolute's "timeless" character. For pluralists, on the other hand, time remains as real as anything, and nothing in the universe is great or static or eternal enough not to have some history. But the world that each of us feels most intimately at home with is that of beings with histories that play into our history, whom we can help in their vicissitudes even as they help us in ours. This satisfaction the absolute denies us; we can neither help nor hinder it, for it stands outside of history. It surely is a merit in a philosophy to make the very life we lead seem real and earnest. Pluralism, in exorcising the absolute, exorcises the great de-realizer of the only life we are at home in, and thus redeems the nature of reality from essential foreignness. Every end, reason, motive, object of desire or aversion, ground of sorrow or joy that we feel is in the world of finite multifariousness, for only in that world does anything really happen, only there do events come to pass. (James 1909)

The elements at issue here, most notably "history" and "events," provide us with images of conflict. Wherever something happens, there is resistance. Sometimes resistance emerges from material elements in nature (forces of nature), other times from anthropomorphic elements (resistance originating from other humans). In this sense, the events in the sublunary world are characterized by conflict. The images or imaginal representations that emerge in narratives to deal with conflict are those I would like to call conflict chronotopes. In its most extreme form, the conflict chronotope can be found in anti-idyllic narratives: legends about mysterious anomalies, tragedies about an unfortunate concurrence of circumstances, and (in less ambitious narratives) anecdotes or novellas that tell "something new." In long-drawn-out narratives, the conflict chronotope creates adventure scenes or (psychological) situations of crisis. Sometimes this type of action-space chronotope takes the shape of an idealized state of dehumanization (Dante's *Inferno*) or a behavior warranting a fight (the evil forces in the adventure stories mapped by Campbell and Propp). Sometimes it appears as a negative state that needs to be overcome (the futility of the picaro in rascal stories, the labyrinthine confusion and threat in horror stories) or as an unfavorable result of decisions already taken (the dehumanized deformations of heroes and heroines in tragedies).

A chronotope is called a conflict chronotope when it meets two conditions. The first is that time needs to be integrated in movements that conflict with the movement of the chronotope's center: the hero or heroine and his or her goals (or "goal-directed plans," which Herman mentioned [2005, 83]). Therefore, it can be argued that the temporal heart of the conflict chronotope is the adventure. In the literal sense of the word, the notion of "adventure" refers to events that are contingent, that befall us; they are adventitious, "come to" the individual (*advenire*) and are parried by equally adventurous counteractions. Because of this concept of time, the conflict chronotope is thematically arranged with anomalies and the disturbance of peace. Sometimes Tyche favors the adventurous person, and sometimes she disfavors him or her; in any case, it is Tyche who is responsible for people having good or bad luck. This is most evident in adventure stories, as we know them from nineteenth-century novels (see the works analyzed in Klotz 1979) or chivalric romances.

At midnight there descended from the rafters suddenly a lance, as with the intention of pinning the knight through the flanks to the coverlet and the white sheets where he lay. To the lance there was attached a pennon all ablaze. The coverlet, the bedclothes, and the bed itself all caught fire at once. And the tip of the lance passed so close to the knight's side that it cut the skin a little, without seriously wounding him. Then the knight got up, put out the fire and, taking the lance, swung it in the middle of the hall, all this without leaving his bed; rather did he lie down again and slept as securely as at first. (Chrétien De Troyes 1914)

The conflict chronotope in an adventure novel revolves around a character becoming the plaything of chance events that either support or obstruct him or her in performing his or her task. In this narrative, the character is subjected to a pattern of time "which consists of the most immediate units—moments, hours, days—snatched at random from the temporal process" (Bakhtin 1986, 11). Ian Fleming's James Bond stories, for example, are composed of episodes in which the hero faces and overcomes obstacles popping up out of nowhere only to integrate them in during the course of the entire project (the elimination of a usurper). It is striking to see how in this concept of time, unlike in that of Aion, time is measured by the standard of human intentions; time provides the fulfillment of intentions or the series of obstacles that impede those intentions. Even if Tyche is often represented as fate (or as any other metaphysical body or agent referring to the supernatural cause of chance), she remains a force on a human scale. Even if chance is deified, as is frequently the case in ancient cultures (see the Greek tragedies), the effects it brings about are invariably *menschliche, allzu menschliche* [human, all too human] phenomena.

In many stories, adventure and chance occur on a social level, where they take the form of *meetings*. Paul Eluard, attacking metaphysical theories of chance, offers a sharp description of this tendency of conflict chronotopes: "There is no such thing as chance; there are only meetings." It is the notion of meeting that contains the second condition a chronotope must meet in order to be called a conflict chronotope: the space in which meetings occur must be an open space where the time of chance can unfold. It goes without saying that this space must be situated outside the isolated space of the equilibrium chronotope. The reason for this is evident—if the space were fenced off, then it would preclude any surprise and a meeting would be reduced to the mere recognition of what is already familiar. This, in turn, explains why the space of the conflict chronotope is protected by the god of travelers and strangers, the deity of people who are on their way, on the road: Hermes. The character ruling the conflict chronotope is a stranger who exits the boundary of his own home and sees new, surprising aspects of reality emerging beyond the threshold—his doorstep, so to speak. Consequently, Bakhtin has rated the phenomenon of the meeting as one of the most important components of narrative art. The meeting is one of the most crucial action-space chronotopes of narratives:

> Quite frequently in literature the chronotope of meeting fulfills architec-
> tonic functions: it can serve as an opening, sometimes as a culmination, even
> as a denouement (a finale) of the plot. A meeting is one of the most ancient
> devices for structuring a plot in the epic (and even more so in the novel).
> (Bakhtin 1981a, 98)

In the final paragraphs of his study of chronotopes Bakhtin discusses the chronotope of the "meeting," which he takes to denote the spatial openness with which characters in conflict chronotopes are confronted. In the text, he focuses his attention on the series of unforeseen circumstances that cross a character's path. Bakhtin argues that the "time of adventure" assumes the concrete form of a series of meetings. Traditional adventure stories, for instance, are typically subdivided in episodes. Each of these contains an altering spatial constellation and nature of the meeting. Episodes that highlight unsuccessful or failed meetings are also signifi-cant: in the second book of *Ephesiaka*, the seeker-hero continually arrives too late, watching his beloved slip through his fingers over and over again. Other episodes rely on the failure to recognize that which is familiar. A meeting can fail because a character wrongly assesses an antagonist or fails to see through a disguise. The misgivings or errors between characters (highly significant in the comedy of errors and sentimental melodrama) can equally be labeled as failed meetings.

Most of the examples mentioned here may indeed originate from the world of the adventure story,[18] yet it is imperative to consider conflict chronotopes to be an essential component of all narratives. In modern literature, the part played by the meeting is often taken by conflicts that imply crises and situations of doubt. For this purpose, the narrator often selects locations symbolizing the character's inse-curity. In his discussion of Dostoevsky, Bakhtin introduces the threshold chrono-tope to illustrate the idea of crisis in the author's work. The most crucial moments in Dostoevsky's work unfold on a doorstep, an entrance, a staircase, or a hallway, where "the chronotope of *crisis* and *break* in a life" unfolds (Bakhtin 1981a, 248; Bakhtin's italics).[19] In addition, Dostoevsky picks out meeting places (the salon, the reception hall, and the dining room) that are easily turned into a battleground for catastrophes and scandals. The center of this space also holds "the threshold":

> The word "threshold" itself already has a metaphorical meaning in every day
> usage (together with its literal meaning), and is connected with the breaking
> point of a life, the moment of crisis, the decision that changes a life (or the

indecisiveness that fails to change a life, the fear to step over the threshold). (Bakhtin 1981a, 248)

At certain crucial moments in modern stories—and this will matter when I define dialogical plot-spaces—characters must make decisions about the direction their actions should take or about the object of their intentions. In Bakhtin's view, these are "unique moments," which are bound up with the spatial image of the threshold. These deciding moments constitute—figuratively speaking—threshold moments in the characters' lives. The space in which they experience these moments are also places where people choose between inside and outside (the door-step) or where they happen to be "on their way" (such as a corridor leading from a secure location to an insecure or strange location).

Earlier, I may have labeled adventure, obstacle, doubt, or crisis as "conflicts," yet this does not in the least imply that conflict chronotopes only concern negative experiences. Central to my definition of conflict is the notion of chance or contingency, as applied in epistemology: "the mixture, or, as Cournot said, the interference of independent causal chains" (Piaget 1967, 616). Apart from the conflict chronotopes that create tension and crisis, other chronotopes reveal meetings to be of a very stimulating nature. A meeting with a character offering support to the hero or heroine could also rightfully be labeled discordant or conflict-related. Fairytales, for example, contain scenes (mostly situated on a mountain or at an open spot in the woods) depicting the hero or heroine during an encounter with a character who offers a helping hand. The first episodes of an adventure plot frequently produce a supporting tool that acquires meaning or demonstrates its use in later adventures. *The Queen Bee* by the Brothers Grimm has fine examples of tools woven into a narrative; other examples of tools include ring-mail received from the elves, the illuminating flask of the woodland elves, the spy gadgets presented to Bond by Q, and so forth. In later episodes the helping hands make an unexpected reappearance or the commissioning authority comes to the rescue. When the going gets tough, the *tougher* indeed get going: *Cinderella's* fairy arrives in time to take away the prince's doubts; M conveniently slips Bond some satellite pictures. Strictly speaking, the positive, stimulating meetings do not involve any crises. Nevertheless, they are surprising and coincidental chance events that display the structure of a conflict chronotope.

From Idealistic to Realistic Conflict Chronotopes

As is the case with equilibrium chronotopes, the outlook of conflict chronotopes varies depending on the worldviews. In the course of Western culture's development, and pertaining to this perspectival variance, a certain evolution can be observed to have heavily influenced the creation of images of conflict. I am referring to the growing influence of biblical religions. According to the religious historian

Mircea Eliade, this influence was reinforced by the excessive celebration of individualism that has marked Western culture since the Renaissance.[20] The way in which the Jewish-Christian civilization thinks about contingent events in this world is very different from the Greek perception of time, still evident in the writings of Plotinus, who inspired Augustine. As I have said earlier, Plotinus's thought perfectly illustrates the idea of the equilibrium chronotope. It also happens to contain an interesting view on conflict chronotopes. In spite of his tendency to look down on worldly conflicts, they nonetheless play an important part in his worldview. They are, in fact, symptoms of general decay because they clearly indicate a loss of perfection (the *proodos* or emanation), although by nature they are oriented toward the superior and eternal sphere. Indeed, Plotinus considers worldly conflicts as intermediary stages that aspire to return (*epistrofè*) to the state of harmony and equilibrium. It is the human species in particular that seeks harmony and tries to attain the ideal state of equilibrium by doing away with the difference, chaos, diversity, and turmoil that characterize the world of senses. The orientation of worldly processes on the superior world is eschatological, in the literal sense of the word: human aspirations in this conflicting reality are directed toward the eschaton, the ultimate moment of union with the eternal and the timeless. As mortals, we have only one genuine object: the value of ideal, universal, and a priori given entities (absolute values, principles, states of blissful happiness, ideal forms of community).

Plotinus's teachings offer a good indication of the extent to which "regularity" in Greek idealistic philosophy of time represents the ultimate criterion for contemplating temporal phenomena. Time is conceived in an absolutist fashion. This is the reason why conflicts in the material world were deemed to be illusions or moments in a larger circular process. When considered from this point of view, conflicts are merely circumstantial. They are nothing more than chance mishaps, setbacks in the universe. Christianity and Judaism shift the emphasis away from the Greek absolutist vision of time, whereupon Western culture starts drifting away from a condescending attitude toward worldly conflicts. It borrows the eschatological idea that the superior world is in fact timeless, but it no longer accepts the view that the inferior world is merely circumstantial. According to Ernst Cassirer in the second volume of *Philosophy of Symbolic Forms* (1925), monotheistic religions are a crucial factor in the shift from one worldview to another. "The emergence of the idea of pure monotheism," he writes, "represents an important turning point in the religious attitude toward time" (Cassirer 1975, 119). In a long quotation from another famous neo-Kantian philosopher, Hermann Cohen (*Die Religion der Vernunft aus den Quellen des Judentums*, 1919), Cassirer asserts that the religious consciousness of the prophets mark the emergence of a different philosophy of time.

> Time becomes future and only future. Past and present are submerged in this time of the future. This return to time is the purest idealization. Be-

fore this idea, all existence vanishes. The existence of man is transcended in this future being. . . . What Greek intellectualism could not create, prophetic monotheism succeeded in creating. History in the Greek consciousness is synonymous with knowledge as such. Hence for the Greeks history is oriented solely toward the past. The Prophet, however, is a seer, not a scholar. . . . Prophets are the idealists of history. Their seerdom created the concept of history as the being of the future. (Cohen 1919, as quoted in Cassirer 1975, 120)

A second step in this evolution is formed by the philosophy of time within Christianity. The change can be explained by the metaphysical significance of the Messiah and the implied moral consequences. Because the divine is incarnated as a son of mortal human beings, it exposes itself to the everyday contingencies in the sublunary world. In the most explicit manner, this worldview has become a feature of Christianity. Christ's life is a concatenation of obstacles (pharisees, sinners, merchants, followers, Romans, the disabled, the doubting or incredulous apostles, etc.) culminating in the conflict chronotope of the passion story. As a result, Christian thought takes a different position toward conflicts. An appropriate summary of this new attitude is given by Georges Maertens in the following quotation:

Not only is the Word born of God, as the Neoplatonists, among others, say, but the Word has also become man, which is why the unchanging God has assumed time; this is indeed the reason why an entirely different relationship between time and eternity has come into being, making it truly possible to go through the former toward the latter. (1965, 114)[21]

It was Augustine who took on the task of laying the foundation for a genuine philosophical explication of this conception of time. He is the architect of a realistic eschatology that is directed toward adjusting Plotinus's idealistic eschatology. Although Augustine entirely follows the Greek view with regard to equilibrium chronotopes (and the ideas of repetition and eschaton), his view of the human mortal (as the other-than-the-Divine and the counterpart of repetition) deviates from the idealistic worldview of antiquity.[22] His philosophy is the first to view history as a problem in such a way that it can be considered emblematic of the manner in which realistic stories handle conflict.

Augustine's Christian thought propounds regularity as the ultimate ideal, but now regularity must be won or gained. It is, from the Creator's perspective, a matter of merit. In other words, regularity becomes a concept of time that is relative to human consciousness. It is one element in a dualistic philosophy of time; apart from the concept of time central to Plotinus's monism, that is, the perpetuity of Aion, there is now room for an equally valuable concept of time representing the human point of view: finiteness. Providence (the symbol of regularity, the force that provides structure and order in the world) remains a prime mover in the universe; however, as a consequence of our fall from grace, we, human mortals, no longer inhabit a world ruled by providence. We must do our time in the sublunary world and submit temporarily to the laws of this finite world. For Christianity, the empirical world, where philosophers such as Plato saw eternal laws and other regularities, is an irregular world far from God. This is why Christian thought makes much of conflicts that are unsolvable or have no apparent solution. Perfection can only be achieved by a model human mortal; only a saint, resembling Christ in his holiness, succeeds in transcending the world of conflicts to enter the world of harmony.

The Jewish-Christian view of the "world of contingencies" runs counter to a long tradition of idealistically conceiving conflict chronotopes. In Greek tragedy, Tyche is fate indicating the will of the gods. Thus, the conflicts in the art of tragedy are direct references to universal values and truths. This also applies to the classic epic where the conflict between Achilles and Agamemnon takes shape as a battle between two principles: honor and authority. In addition to this, the epic heroes and heroines are frequently representatives of the super- or transtemporal world sent into the sublunary world. In *Anatomy of Criticism*, Frye analyzes the hero of German epics as follows: "The hero of romance is analogous to the mythical Messiah or deliverer who comes from an upper world, and his enemy is analogous to the demonic powers of a lower world" (1973, 187). Supertemporal agents who create conflict are also present in the Greek "adventure novel of ordeal" (Bakhtin 1981a, 86–111):

> Moments of adventuristic time occur at those points when the normal course of events, the normal, intended or purposeful sequence of life's events is interrupted. These points provide an opening for the intrusion of nonhuman forces—fate, gods, villains—and it is precisely these forces, and not the heroes, who in adventure-time take all the initiative. (Bakhtin 1981a, 95)

Dante, for his part, conceptualizes conflicts in God's creational plan from a Christian perspective. In his view, Fortuna (Inferno VII) is an instrument of God's providence. The conflicts and gifts that befall him in *Divina Commedia* are supertemporal ordeals for his mortal soul (Köhler 1973, 30). In the religious epic and tragedy of the modern period (Joost van den Vondel, John Milton), the epic's idealistic view of conflicts is blended with the medieval idea of providence. In van den Vondel's *Adam in Ballingschap* (*Adam in Exile*), Adam and Eve face trials that comprise a test within a creational plan for the universe. The conflicts faced by knights in the late medieval romance are also trials pointing to universality. The knights in the Arthurian romances undertake campaigns of conquest in order to regain the superior (values of the creational plan for the universe) from the inferior, thereby elevating the contingent onto the level of the universal. Consequently, they are not confronted with a human evil, but with Evil, as such.

> In view of the fact that what comes to him also really befalls [bechances] him, the protagonist of the Arthurian romance sets out on a quest for *aventure–adventura.* . . . In the adventure, the courtly knight's quest integrates chance in a universalizing historical context, which culminates in the chivalrous eschatology of the Grail romance. (Köhler 1973, 29)[23]

In fact, mythical obstacles such as dragons and other thoroughly evil creatures function as instruments to put forward the Good, universal values and truths. These idealistic conflict chronotopes continue to recur up until the Romantic movement. Their heroes and heroines will remain as individuals who are doomed to be confronted with conflicts imposed on them by the super- or translunary world (Bakhtin 1981a, 95).

In narrative art, the idealistic view of conflicts has gradually been countered by more realistically conceived conflict chronotopes. The history of Western narrative art indeed shows a growing interest in conflicts that are modeled after "everyday problems." Realistic conflict chronotopes acknowledge Tyche to be a force operating in the empirical world and providing series of "material" accidents or coincidences (which are not associated with universal ideals). In these cases, the accidental is no longer an illusion or feeble extraction of the real world (of eternal values and truths). Instead, it is a phenomenon belonging to everyday life. The universe in which material coincidences occupy a central position is an open system that cannot be entirely decoded by means of a supertemporal key. This, however, does not entail that moral codes and universal truths vanish from narratives. They are still presented (by way of equilibrium chronotopes), yet they are contrasted with contingency-infused conflict chronotopes.[24]

As far as antiquity is concerned, we can situate the first appearance of these realistic conflict chronotopes in the genre labeled by Bakhtin as the "travel novel" (1986) or the "adventure novel of everyday life" (1981a, 111–29). The relative concept of time is displayed in a series of meaningful conflicts, such as confrontations with violent and unreliable individuals whose actions are solely driven by self-interest. Indeed, the realistic worldview manifests itself very early in Western cultural history. Certainly, it is difficult to pinpoint an exact temporal location in history because both worldviews usually coexist and frequently even "co-star" in the same narratives. Nonetheless, we can assume contingencies and everyday obstacles to be the focus of ever-increasing attention in later forms of Western narrative culture.

The first traces of this can be detected in the work of Dante. In his view, the cause of the eschatological quest is based in rational self-consciousness. The human mortal must truly want to see the order (which explains the strong emphasis put on knowledge in the evocation of the eighth circle of heaven) and be ready to repent. The definitive breakthrough of chance being accepted as a prime mover of the universe is a fact in the work of Boccaccio and the art of the novella. In the modern era, chance truly acquires autonomy. For a medieval person thinking exclusively in metaphysical terms, Fortuna's power is a given but merely an accidental one, inferior to the substantial force of the creator, in any case. For the realist, the world consists of individuals who are acting rationally or in a voluntaristic manner and are confronted with a series of blind forces. Especially from the Renaissance (sixteenth century) onward, narrative art appears to grow sensitive to "the flow of historical time" (Bakhtin 1981a, 244).[25]

A good example is Shakespeare's *Othello*. In the course of the play, the call for "proof" is almost obsessively recurrent. Finally, proof is found in an accidentally lost handkerchief, owing to Iago's ingenuity. Chance, coincidence, and misfortune are blind forces of nature to Shakespeare. They represent the opposite of providence and, as such, are forces actually capable of either helping or thwarting the individual will. Moreover, with Shakespeare, the seed is sown for the idea that human passions are beyond control because they are subject to chance. Passions are blind, fateful forces that ask for control and composure but will not allow themselves to be ruled by a single form of regularity. In the Renaissance, the confrontation of the individual with nature and the passions that inhabit him or her takes the form of a journey along a path of life that attracts a swarm of contingencies. It could be argued that the psychologizing of the conflict chronotope paved the way for modern literature, especially if we consider how the hand of fate remained in full force in the centuries following the Renaissance. In Bakhtin's view, the nineteenth-century novel will exploit the realistic conflict chronotopes to such an extent that no room will seem to be left for equilibrium chronotopes. Even the interiorized forms of equilibrium, which he calls the "sublimated idylls," will succumb under the weight of a culture ruled by chance. In the nineteenth-century novel,

> the issue is primarily one of overturning and demolishing the worldview and psychology of the idyll, which proved increasingly inadequate to the new capitalist world. In most such cases there is no philosophical sublimation of the idyll. We get a picture of the breakdown of provincial idealism under forces emanating from the capitalist center. (Bakhtin 1981a, 234)[26]

Eventually this evolution will end with the tales of chance we know from the modern novel, for example, surrealist works. According to Erich Köhler, the increasing social complexity and insecurity of historical reality would lead to artists experiencing still greater difficulty to decode the signs of the necessary in the real. Probability has ceased to bow for meaningful necessity. Teleology, even that of sober-minded rationality, became vain delusion in the face of the omnipresence of what is possible, which leaves everything open to arbitrary chance. (1973, 78–79)[27]

In conclusion, I would like to briefly recapitulate in one simple image the contrast between idealistic and realistic conflict chronotopes; Bakhtin considers both from the perspective of the contrast between "the chronotope of the miraculous world" (1981a, 155) and the chronotope of the road. In the epic, the chivalric romance, and the Greek sophist love novel, our imaginal representation of the world is still that of "an 'alien world' separated from one's own native land by sea and distance" (1981a, 245). In the ancient travel novel and the picaresque novel, a more concrete chronotope is highlighted: the "high road winding through one's native land" (Bakhtin 1981a, 165). After all, the road is the place where meetings acquire the nature of everyday events, where fictional events unfold as part of the variable and essentially topical world of the familiar environment.

The road had been profoundly, intensely etched by the flow of historical time, the traces and signs of time's passage, by markers of the era. . . . The road is always one that passes through familiar territory, and not through some exotic alien world . . . ; it is the sociohistorical heterogeneity of one's own country that is revealed and depicted. (Bakhtin 1981a, 244, 245)[28]

Events in an alien, wonderful world have the power to unfold anywhere (James Bond is equally active in the Sahara as he is at the North Pole without the conflict ever changing in essence; see Bakhtin 1981a, 100). Events in a realistic context, however, adopt a unique meaning enabling them to express an existential and historical problem. In choosing conflict chronotopes that are situated on the familiar path of life, the novel selects strategies that are appropriate "for portraying events governed by chance" (Bakhtin 1981a, 243–44). In other words, Bakhtin links the alternative conflict chronotopes to a new worldview, to another perception of chance events and of the space in which they unfold. The conflict chronotopes influenced by realistic chronotopes are situated at the crossroads of everyday life.

Interaction Between Equilibrium and Conflict: Eschaton and Kairos

Only certain groups of stories have an exclusive preference for particular types of chronotopes and action-spaces. This is the case for myths and anecdotes, which seem to display a more or less exclusive preference for equilibrium and conflict chronotopes respectively. In the majority of stories, however, the narrators attempt to establish a balance between both. This was the case in Greek religion.

The French anthropologist and historian Jean-Pierre Vernant detects in the alternation of equilibrium and conflict chronotopes proof of a system that derives its meaning exactly from the interaction between the two. Referring to the two spatial categories of imagination, Hestia and Hermes, he gets to the crux of Western narrative culture:

> If the two divinities form a pair in Greek religious consciousness, it is because they are situated on a similar level, because their action applies to the same domain of the real, because they assume cognate functions. As far as Hestia is concerned, there is no doubt whatsoever: her meaning is transparent, her role strictly defined. Because her destiny is to reside, forever immobile, at the heart of the domestic space, Hestia implies, in harmony and contrast with it, the swift divinity ruling over the space of all travelers. To Hestia, the inside, the enclosed, the immutable, the human community withdrawing to itself; to Hermes, the outside, the openness, the mobility, the contact with the other than oneself. (Vernant 1963, 15)[29]

Hestia and Hermes are mutually dependent in narratives, and they subdivide the storyworld into two basic components: on the one hand, action-spaces that stage an "inside" and represent closeness, immobility, and hominess; on the other hand, action-spaces that stage an "outside" and represent openness, mobility, and meeting. These components can be endlessly reiterated. Sometimes it means that peaceful images come into being, and sometimes the representations suggest turmoil. The smaller we make the examined components, the greater the variation we discover. Occasionally, even discordant images are found in equilibrium chronotopes just as harmonious images prove to be implicitly permeated by conflict.

This is the reason why the study of chronotopes can never be the key to convincing interpretations of texts. This sort of research can yield little more than a catalogue of contrasts; apart from this, an interpretation of texts based on subjective reconstructions of imaginal elements can hardly be more than some variant of traditional hermeneutics. Instead, the power of this method of inquiry is to be found in its capacity of enabling us to make general statements about a given narrative culture. As was previously shown, the study of action-space chronotopes allows us to retrace different types (for example, external and psychological forms of equilibrium and conflict) and demonstrate or illustrate the influence of worldviews on concrete events in a narrative.

An analysis of the rhythm at which regularity and chance alternate in a narrative is of greater significance than a meticulous study of chronotopes. The patterns of alternating between repetition and difference can indeed vary considerably. By mapping the types of variation, the study of imagination can be used as a tool for delineating groups of texts or genres. A researcher may indeed achieve astonishing results provided he or she leaves aside the rhythm of alternation or variance on a micro-level (from one action-space to another) and is intent on turning images stored as larger portions in the memory into the objects of inquiry. One fine example would be the successive instances of conflict in adventure tales (mostly involving three major moments), which can be singled out and arranged together in order to examine how this larger chronotope of conflict relates to the equilibrium chronotopes (the state of peace and quiet at the beginning and the end of the story). This method may allow the researcher to avoid the risk of getting lost in the overwhelming multitude of events. All he or she must do is set the distinct goal of singling out the big "movements" that create the dynamics of the plot-space. Whatever the extent to which the rhythm of a narrative is interrupted, each narrative is usually composed of different tempos that can be compared to analogous modulations in musical works (think, for example, of the allegro, andante, and allegretto tempos in concertos). Bakhtin refers to this in his analysis of the conflict chronotopes in Greek adventure novels.

> It is not mandatory, of course, for an entire novel to be constructed in adventure-time of the Greek type. One need only have a certain admixture of these time-elements to other time-sequences for its special accompanying effects to appear. (1981a, 96)

Indeed, it is striking to observe that the nature and the position of conflict chronotopes are of overriding importance in the search for stereotyped movements. Great differences are usually rooted in the manner of introducing the conflict chronotopes. In traditional stories (which I have referred to as teleological), the position of the conflict chronotope in the totality of the narrative's tension curve enables the researcher to define different types. Additionally, it is the nature of conflict chronotopes that is responsible for establishing two sorts of plot-spaces. If those chronotopes represent external obstacles, then the narrative will create a teleological plot-space. When this is the case, it involves a distribution similar to that of concertos: equilibrium and conflict are linked to each other in a strict fashion by ascribing to them a fixed place in the plot-space, where they can develop their own tempo. The final moment, the eschaton, plays a crucial part in this. If the conflict chronotopes are mainly of a psychological nature, then a network of conflicting situations comes into existence. The plot evolves within this system through a series of psychological actions and reactions: a desire or an intention, a feeling of frustration or fear. Because of the fact that the different junctions in the network intercommunicate (or interreact), this type of plot-space can rightfully be called *dialogical*. The movements are not so much situated between juxtaposed elements as they are at the junctions of the dialogical network. I will later call the temporal moment occupying a central position at those junctions the moments of kairos.

HESTIA-AION AND HERMES-TYCHE IN TELEOLOGICAL PLOT-SPACES

The alternation between conflict and equilibrium receives a relatively taut structure in the majority of stories in Western narrative culture. In his text on Hestia and Hermes, Vernant stresses the role attributed by Greek religion to Hestia:

> We can say that the pair Hermes-Hestia expresses in its polarity the tension that marks the archaic representation of space; space demands a center, an unmoving point of privileged value, from where orientation is possible and from whence directions, all differences can be qualitatively defined; but at the same time, the space presents itself as a site of movement, which implies a possibility of transition and passage from one point to any other. (1963, 15)[30]

In teleological narratives Hestia and Aion function as a center, a home base, a pause. They are the goal (the telos) of the narrative and they impose their will on the conflict chronotopes. Conflicts are merely detours: they are the peripeteias of a hero or heroine who is trying to return home by way of a long voyage. The movements taking place in the open space (the outside) are intermediary stages and phenomena of passage. The pattern can be observed in most forms of popular narrative art:

> Narrative often displays itself in terms of an end which functions as its (partial) condition, its magnetizing force, its organizing principle. (Prince 1982, 157)[31]

The clearest proof of the final moment's magnetic force is found in the success of narratives with a pronounced happy ending. Lotman argues that our fondness for happy endings can be retraced to our capability to recognize in storyworlds an evaluation of the world outside of the narrative: "that's why a good or bad ending is so significant for us: it attests not only to the conclusion of some plot, but also to the construction of the world as a whole" (1977, 216). In the happy ending, to phrase it differently, the heart of the narrative world is asserted. All action-spaces merely seem to be satellites circling around this central point, which is in fact the plot's final moment. The corresponding mental image could be called a teleological plot-space. The reader gradually figures out how to isolate the pieces in order to mentally put together the totality, seeing to it that every piece is assigned its proper position on the linear plotline; the events, in other words, are put in a straitjacket. For Aristotle, this image of the plot-space was an evidential fact. In the ninth paragraph of *Poetics*, Aristotle states that the core of poetry includes the fact that stories show how events are interconnected and provide "tension" through this interconnectedness (1929, 51b 33). A story generates most of its tension from the very beginning by making references to the end. While, and after, the story is consumed, beginning and end are interlinked in a spatial construction that can be called the story arc. Aristotle famously argued the following:

> Now, according to our definition Tragedy is an imitation of an action that is complete, and whole, and of a certain magnitude; for there may be a whole that is wanting in magnitude. A whole is that which has a beginning, a middle, and an end. A beginning is that which does not itself follow anything by causal necessity, but after which something naturally is or comes to be. An end, on the contrary, is that which itself naturally follows some other thing, either by necessity, or as a rule, but has nothing following it. A middle is that which follows something as some other thing follows it. A well constructed plot, therefore, must neither begin nor end at haphazard, but conform to these principles. Again, a beautiful object, whether it be a living organism or any whole composed of parts, must not only have an orderly arrangement of parts, but must also be of a certain magnitude; for beauty depends on magnitude and order. (1929, 50b, 23 and 24)

Behind the alternation of equilibrium and conflict, behind this little dance of Hestia (Aion) and Hermes (Tyche), Aristotle detects a structure. The story arc provides structure to the narrative and does this in such a way that equilibrium and conflict become mutually dependent. In a comedy, this is done by situating the equilibrium at the end of the story arc. In a tragedy, the choice is to direct the story arc straight toward a fatal conflict. This definition of the "perfect plot" is based on an eschatological philosophy of time. The teleological tendency contained in the story arc ensures that the final moment gains extra importance. The final moment becomes the telos, the goal, and also the intention of the story. It could be argued that Aristotle's four guardian gods of the action-space during their interaction (the "French quadrille" of the two pairs: Hestia and Aion, Hermes and Tyche) generate a new concept of time: the eschaton. They obey the rhythm imposed by the final moment and continually force the events along the right, teleologically justified lines.

Because multiple forms of eschatology are possible, the group of teleological chronotopes will be diverse. Following on the discussion of idealistic and realistic conflict chronotopes, narratives embedding a conflict chronotope into an idealistic eschatology could be said to presuppose a situation of equilibrium (as would be required by the philosophy of Plato and Plotinus). The equilibrium is broken—the scales are tilted—because the "outside" infiltrates the "inside" (evil forces beleaguer the peaceful home base). Because an emissary of a superior order (the hero or heroine) undertakes a journey to the "outside" (the inhospitable world of conflicts), the narrative ends with a restored equilibrium. In the next chapter I will call this type of plot-space, used by the largest group of narratives in Western narrative culture,[32] a *mission chronotope.* The hero or heroine undertaking or leading the mission would typically be almost immune to conflicts. Because the hero or heroine is to such a large extent permeated by higher values (as was shown in the quoted scene of Chrétien de Troyes' *Lancelot, or, the Knight of the Cart*), he or she is the chosen one over whom conflicts have no hold.

Another view of conflicts can be found in a second type of teleological chronotope. Here the eschaton is reconsidered according to the patterns of realistic eschatology. It is integrated within a dualist philosophy of time modeled after Augustine. Although the equilibrium chronotopes (the happy ending, for instance) are often barely different from those in the previous type, there is a marked difference at the level of conflict chronotopes. They form the point of departure: an "inferior" figure finds itself in a state of decay (for example, Lazarillo is put out by his mother to beg; Lucius is transformed into a donkey owing to his curiosity; Jonathan Harker is forced by Dracula to remain in his keep) and regenerates in the course of the narrative into a "superior" figure (Lazarillo makes his entrance into citizenship; Lucius becomes a priest of Isis; Harker has a family). Within this plot-space, the eschatological development is constructed in such a way that the conflict chronotopes' meaning is preserved. The elevated individual escapes the conflicts a richer man or woman because these conflicts help him or her to achieve a higher goal. In the next chapter I will call these plot-spaces *regeneration chronotopes* by referring to the picaresque narrative art and the Greek travel novel. In these stories, the eschaton is the result of a regeneration process, not of a mission.

There is a popular variant of the regeneration chronotope in which the process is reversed: the superior figure emerges from the conflicts a richer person, despite the fact that these conflicts have downgraded him or her to an inferior level of existence. These tragic stories end with a conflict situation, and, consequently, the corresponding plot-space can be called a *degradation chronotope*, where the eschaton is a conflict between an individual and higher powers, in which the latter must taste defeat. It may come as a surprise that tragic stories generate a teleologically organized plot-space, even though it really is a linear line with a high degree of goal-directedness. The eschaton constitutes nonachievement of the goal: the hero or heroine's actions actually are entirely heterotelic. Nevertheless, the goal determines the course of the narrative. Because of the fact that the higher powers also populate the eschaton, the opposition between the degraded individual and the eternal laws of the universe serves as a "pause" and as the heart of the plot-space.

HESTIA-AION AND HERMES-TYCHE IN DIALOGICAL PLOT-SPACES

A fourth type of plot-space is radically different from the three previously discussed chronotopes. This phenomenon is also in keeping with the discussion of idealistic and realistic conflict chronotopes. The first type of teleological chronotopes heavily paid tribute to the monist philosophy of time (the idealistic eschatology), whereas the second and third one follow the pattern of a dualist philosophy of time (the realistic eschatology). In the fourth type of plot-space, the concept of time becomes "pluralist," in the sense that the term was used by William James. Modern literature presents conflicts in such a way that with regard to a philosophy of time any form of eschatology or absolutism is excluded. This is most evident in the art of the modern novel. In line with the argument developed here, Bakhtin mentions that Dostoevsky introduced a new type of narrative in Western narrative culture. Leaving aside the issue or whether or not the Russian novelist was indeed the first to introduce this new type,[33] and granting that he was, in any case, one of the first to consistently apply a new strategy of imagination, Dostoevsky's intervention consists of having his characters tell stories about equilibrium and conflict. Indeed, the novelist breaks away from the tendency to consider characters as building blocks of a plot-space that aspires to a totalizing image.

> In his works a hero appears whose voice is constructed exactly like the voice of the author himself in a novel of the usual type. A character's word about himself and his world is just as fully weighted as the author's word usually is; it is not subordinated to the character's objectified image as merely one of his characteristics, nor does it serve as a mouthpiece for the author's voice. It possesses extraordinary independence in the structure of the work. (Bakhtin 1984a, 7)

In Dostoevsky's view, characters are no longer objects ("fixed elements in the author's design"). The plot-space is no longer a combination of "finalized images of people in the unity of a monologically perceived and understood world," but a

> plurality of equally-valid consciousnesses, each with its own world. In Dostoevsky's novels, the ordinary pragmatics of the plot play a secondary role and perform special and unusual functions. The ultimate clamps that hold his novelistic world together are a different sort entirely; the fundamental event revealed through his novel does not lend itself to an ordinary pragmatic interpretation at the level of the plot. (Bakhtin 1984a, 7)

The upshot of introducing centers of consciousness of equal value is indeed that every character will singly form a world. In fact, the feeling of hominess—the spatial center in eschatological narratives (see Hestia in Vernant's analysis)—

ceases to be the most important point of reference. The characters continue to
long for a pause and a haven, but the pause is now situated *within* their world. The
world surrounding the characters has the complete markings of a world thematically arranged with Hermes.

The integral image of the plot-space does not correspond to a teleologically
progressing storyline that aspires to pause; instead, it corresponds to the image
of a restless multivocal dialogue. The dialogical chronotope, which Dostoevsky's
work installs in the reader's consciousness, consists in a network of junctions of
consciousness that is continuously shifting, as if it were making a journey. Because
the work presents a relationship of tension between psychological centers of action, it requires the reader to develop a dialogical image of the plot-space. The
recipient may be free to bypass such a reaction. *Crime and Punishment* can certainly
be read as an exciting crime story or as a bittersweet tragedy, yet the communication is robbed of quality if the dialogical imagery is forsaken.[34] The first authors
radically choosing the dialogical method went out of their way to explain to their
audience that their work really needed to be read *differently*. Henry James's famous
anecdote about Ivan Turgenev (in his introduction to *The Portrait of a Lady*) can
perhaps shed some light on the matter.[35] As it happened, Turgenev discussed the
central problem of the book, that of narrative imagination, with James. During
the conversation, the former claimed that a fictional world is born out of "the
(re)presentation of one or more characters" that in one way or the other incite the
author's interest. According to Turgenev, the crucial problem with this is finding
a strategy to make these characters enter into a specific interaction. According to
James, Turgenev saw his characters

> subject to the chances, the complications of existence, and saw them vividly,
> but then had to find for them the right relations, those that would most
> bring them out; to imagine, to invent and select and piece together the situa-
> tions most useful and favourable to the sense of the creatures themselves, the
> complications they would be most likely to produce and to feel. "To arrive at
> these things is to arrive at my story," he [Turgenev] said, "and that's the way I
> look for it. The result is that I'm often accused of not having 'story' enough.
> I seem to myself to have as much as I need—to show my people, to exhibit
> their relations with each other; for that is all my measure. If I watch them
> long enough I see them come together, I see them *placed*, I see them engaged
> in this or that act and in this or that difficulty." (2001)

Any summary of stories, where relationships between "thinking, wanting and
feeling" characters have the upper hand, has no other option than to reconstruct a
dialogue. It is striking to see how often summaries of modern novels are structured

around the decisions that must be taken by a character. If a person should want to "plot out" a story by Balzac, Dostoevsky, or James, he or she will soon realize that the only things to hold on to are the descriptions of oppositions between characters and between psychological forces. It is, therefore, necessary to map out the moments that are decisive for the characters, also from their own point of view. As with teleological plot-spaces, these elements can be captured in a complex yet integral image.

> Causal relations between characters in narrative are central to questions about their psychology, motivations, and interactions within the framework of the plot; occasionally they also involve metaphysical issues as well. (Richardson 2005, 48)

The storyworld is at its most visible when a cognitive map is drawn of the options open to the characters in terms of thought and action, of their situations, and of the relationships they entertain with other characters. As was the case with teleological plot-spaces, a mental map is actually being drawn while we are reading. This time, however, it does not concern a map of alternating equilibrium and conflict chronotopes but one of interiorized forms of equilibrium and conflict. The result of this process of cognitive mapping is invariably a network of dialoguing junctions.

As was clear from James's statement that characters are "subject to the risks and the complications of existence," the nature of the conflict chronotopes plays a crucial role in the genesis of dialogical plot-spaces. Because of the fact that Hestia disappears from the storyworlds (Aion and Hestia retreat into the characters' psyche), modern stories will rely heavily on Hermes and Tyche. As was shown above, conflicts in modern literature cease to be used allegorically (the fact is that metaphysical oppositions belong to an eschatological philosophy of time and to the world of eternity). They will now be conceived and perceived as historical, everyday events (Morson and Emerson 1990, 405–13; Morson 1991, 1082–86).

Bakhtin confirms this hypothesis in reference to Dostoevsky because the latter displays a strong preference for conflict chronotopes in which Hermes is "at the doorstep" (or threshold) and Tyche stages moments of crisis. At the threshold, everyday ("historical") events present themselves and leave their marks in all characters' consciousness. The dialogue between characters is fed by the interactions between them and their surroundings. Sometimes these surroundings are other characters with whom a hero or heroine enters into a dialogue; sometimes a hero or heroine's interlocutors consist of entire groups or institutions. Hence, Bakhtin argues, a symbiosis exists between a character's historical environment and a character in isolation. The dialogical chronotope's plot development is indeed typically attached to the psychological dynamics of the characters at issue.

Changes in the hero himself acquire plot significance, and thus the entire plot of the novel is reinterpreted and reconstructed. Time is introduced into man, enters into his very image, changing in a fundamental way the signifi-cance of all aspects of his destiny and life. (Bakhtin 1986, 21)[36]

It is quite possible that the changes within the hero or heroine follow a teleo-logical pattern (and this is often the case), yet the integral image of the narrative changes because of the deciding psychological moments being placed in opposi-tion to each other. Modern stories operate according to relationships of tension between characters, and they show this tension at times when these characters are reacting (feeling, desiring, thinking) psychologically. This explains why the move-ments in the plot-space mainly unfold at isolated moments of time. Consequently, these are exactly the moments that need to be mapped by the recipient.

The network of junctions arising in a dialogical plot-space chronotope bears witness to the pluralistic philosophy of time. The most important developments of time are no longer the movements that progress toward the eschaton, but the movements as they are experienced by the characters. In terms of the philoso-phy of time, the modern novel is a post-Kantian undertaking. The difference be-tween the philosophy of time before and after Kant is beautifully illustrated by a famous phrase from Arthur Schopenhauer, particularly cherished by the French situationists:

Before Kant we were in time; now time is in us. [Vor Kant waren wir in der Zeit, seit Kant ist sie in uns.] (1969, 424.)

Before Kant, monist and dualist concepts of time of an eschatological kind played the leading part. Since Kant, this leading role has been taken by a concept of time that is entirely set on highlighting the power of psychological and subjective abili-ties. Evidently, philosophy did not have to wait for Kant to develop this concept of time. The fact that a realistic eschatology can perfectly be reconciled with re-flections on the psychological forms of time was already obvious from Augustine's teachings and series of teleological writings. However, the sensitivity for a pluralis-tic philosophy of time began noticeably gaining ground in the eighteenth century. This is true for not only philosophy but also narrative culture. The eighteenth-century novel (think of the cobweb spun in many epistolary novels) is certainly a fine example of a narrative form in which attention is not only reserved for the teleological plot but also for the dialogue between pluralistically conceived mo-ments in time. As it turned out, the latter narrative form never have stopped grow-ing in importance during the course of the following centuries.

The pluralistic concept of time dominant in the modern novel is in need of its own proper name. Just as the four guardian gods of the action-space in their teleologically oriented interaction gave birth to the concept of the eschaton, so too the "French quadrille" of Aion-Hestia and Tyche-Hermes should, in this case, lead to a new concept of time. As will become clear further on, the Bergsonian term "duration" proves to be an adequate concept to designate a psychologizing narrative imagination (as well as the dialogue of moments in time arising in it). The fact remains, however, that duration also refers to memory and simultaneity. It is not until the twentieth century that the latter two phenomena will become important in literature. An older term, therefore, seems more appropriate; *kairos* proves to be perfect for pointing out the role of network junctions in the dialogical plot-space. Kairos is ancient Greek for "the right or opportune moment" (and, in this sense, is related to Tyche, a concept heavily favored by modern texts). Even more important is its connotation of "the deciding moment." One of the etymological roots of the concept originates from archery: kairos is the moment at which the opponent is hit on a crucial spot and at a deciding moment. In his *Kaironomia*, discussing this connotation in the context of rhetoric, E. C. White defines a moment of kairos as "a passing instant when an opening appears which must be driven through with force if success is to be achieved" (1984, 13). For the same reason, the term is often used by theologians. Kairos is in fact the moment at which the time of the sublunary and the super- or translunary intersect, temporarily bringing together conflict and equilibrium.[37] Even more fitting in a characterization of narrative imagination are the connotations mentioned by Kermode. Referring to Kierkegaard's existentialism and German philosophy of the 1930s, Kermode states that kairos relates to the deciding moments of existence, moments at which man "senses his position in the middest, desiring these moments of significance which harmonize origin and end" (Kermode 1968, 48). In this sense, the term very neatly corresponds to the emphasis modern novels put on moments of decisions, of crisis (threshold chronotopes).

Kairos time usually is crisis time. Modern literature is frequently concerned with personal crises occurring in borderline situations, those moments at which, according to the existentialist Karl Jaspers, "personal crisis—death, suffering, guilt" enter into a relationship with "the data which constitute its historical determination" (Kermode 1968, 47). From an existential point of view, critical moments point to our *Geworfenheit*—the moment we were thrown into this life for God knows what reason—and at the same time to a fixed end point. Existence, to use Martin Heidegger's words, is a *Sein zum Tode* [Being-toward-death]. During moments of kairos, the individual makes a decision about the way in which he or she will send his personality, shaped by the past, into a new future direction. This kind of philosophy of time, in which the teleological timeline is fully interiorized, handsomely fits the type of narrative imagination I have outlined above. The world of characters, and the temporal movement present in it, makes up the heart of the modern plot-space.

To conclude, I want to point out a final connotation of the concept of kairos. Alain Badiou has recently increased the value of the deciding moments in a

human life, which he explicitly calls kairos moments, to the level of what is at
stake in an "ethics of the good." A human being can remain loyal to or betray a
certain event, even if the moment was not lived consciously or even if the event
did not entail a lucid choice. The extent to which a human being remains loyal
to his decisions determines the moral caliber of his actions. This view of morality
closely resembles that of Dostoevsky and is perfectly in accordance with the other
connotations of kairos.

Once again, it is also a confirmation of the extent to which a change in worldview can influence narrative culture. In literature, an eschatological worldview—
by way of a plot-space chronotope—leads straight to an ethics in which fixed
moral categories are applied. The characters in a teleological plot-space are able to
be told their moral position a priori: cowboys representing the equilibrium chronotope wear a white hat, and the representatives of the evil outside world wear
a black one. In modern texts, in which kairos structures the dominant temporal
movements, a different, more situational ethics is active. The good is defined by
weighing the positions in a specific situation against each other. Because the relationships of force that are held between these positions are not easily analyzed,
kairos, as a famous Greek proverb goes, is always a lack of time:

> «*Chronos estin en ô Kairos, Kairos d'en ô chronos ou polys*»: time is henceforth that
> in which there is kairos (opportunity to act, the right moment, the critical
> instant) and the kairos is that in which there isn't much time. (Castoriadis
> 1975, 292)[38]

Plot-Space and Worldview

Up to this point, I have associated dialogical plot-spaces with modern narratives
and connected the teleological variant with traditional literature. Although this
typological distinction is to some extent legitimate, it should never be pushed
to its extreme. It is probably more prudent to talk about two interpretations or
two methods of understanding narrative imagination. In a sense, and this was
already apparent from my comment regarding the moral dimension of eschaton
and kairos, choosing one or the other entails opting for a certain worldview. In
this concluding section, I want to make explicit the philosophical connotations of
teleological and dialogical plot-spaces.

TRADITIONAL STORY ARCS AND MODERN NETWORKS
In historical surveys and narratological studies, the tautly delineated teleological
plot-space is often placed in opposition to the pluralistic dialogical plot-space.

In this way, the rise of modern literature is often linked to the end of traditional plot-oriented narration and the rise of modern narrative strategies. Manfred Jahn, implicitly referring to Brooks, argues there is a difference between the traditional and the modern view of plot patterns:

> In traditional, plot-oriented texts, the main conflict is usually resolved by marriage, death, or some other aesthetically or morally satisfactory outcome producing a state of equilibrium. Many modern texts, however, lack closure; they may be open ended (Weldon, "Weekend"), simply stop (Hemingway, "The Killers"), conclude enigmatically (Fowles, "The Enigma"), or ambiguously (Wells, "The Country of the Blind"), or even offer alternative endings (Bradbury, "Composition"). (2005, N4.9)

Jahn's term "plot-oriented text" is a frequently used label for traditional texts. It denotes a teleologically constructed plot: all elements collaborate to achieve a set objective. The fact is that the traditional narrative's plot-space can be perfectly described by means of a story arc, as we have learned from traditional scriptwriting classes and the famous triangle of tragedy drawn up by Freytag. Narratives having a well-delineated story arc include those Pavel categorized as idealistic narrative forms (the early form of novel known as the Greek romance, the chivalric romance, *Amadis of Gaul,* and the Baroque adventure novel); their popular heirs (robinsonades, nineteenth-century romantic adventure novels à la Dumas, crime stories, and Hollywood action stories); the older forms of the realistic literary novel (picaresque and gothic); and twentieth-century horror stories or horror thrillers.

The schemas drawn up by structuralist narratologists to plumb the depths of plot mechanisms (for example, Propp's list of narrative functions or Algirdas Julien Greimas' actantial scheme) are particularly applicable to these types of texts. They prove that goal-directedness and succession of discrete actions constitute their very own building blocks. Tzvetan Todorov (who at the end of the 1960s developed a *"grammaire du récit,"* a narrative grammar, in his seminal works; see Todorov 1968 and 1969) and Claude Bremond (1966) have generalized this schema by pointing out that a narrative in its elementary state "stretches" a story arc from a state of balance to a situation of imbalance, which at the end of the narrative bends back to a new or renewed state of balance. Lotman briefly recapitulates the definition of traditional texts by contrasting them with Bakhtin's view of the modern novel.

> In Propp's description, a text gravitates toward panchronic equilibrium: . . . there is only an oscillation around some homeostatic norm (equilibrium—disruption of equilibrium—restoration of equilibrium). In Bakhtin's analysis,

the inevitability of movement, change, and destruction is latent even in the static state of a text. . . . For Propp, the natural domain of a text is the folk tale, but for Bakhtin it is the novel and the play. (1981, 38)

Not only Bakhtin but also the majority of literary theorists sensed that the definition given by structural semiotics failed to cover the vast range of literary texts. They found that applying formalist schemas to the modern novel was not a successful method of analysis (Herman and Vervaeck 2005, 54). Hence, it seemed preferable in the case of modern texts to entirely abort the task of defining the plot-space or, in any case, to discuss the issue exclusively in negative terms. Probably the most distinct choice in favor of conceptual vagueness is found in José Ortega y Gasset's *Notes on the Novel* (1927), where he discusses the "disappearance of the plot":

In its beginnings the plot may have seemed to form its most important part. Later it appeared that what really matters is not the story which is told but that the story, whatever it might be, should be told well. (1948, 63)

"Epics, romances of chivalry, adventure stories, dime novels, serials," on the one hand, are based on an action "which moves as fast as possible toward a conclusion" (Ortega 1948, 80–81). The modern novel, on the other hand, proceeds from very different principles:

The order must be inverted: the action or plot is not the substance of a novel but its scaffolding, its mechanical prop. The essence of the novel—that is to say, of the modern novel with which alone I am here concerned—does not lie in "what happens" but precisely in the opposite: in the personages' pure living, in their being and being thus, above all, in the ensuing milieu. (Ortega 1948, 87)

Ortega's plea in favor of the modern novel is very much in keeping with its tendency to represent the plot-space as the anti-plot or as a non-action-oriented plot. Crane, architect of the Chicago School's neo-Aristotelian literary criticism, introduced the distinction between the "plot of action," on the one hand, and the "plot of character" and "plot of thought," on the other hand. This distinction equally relies on the observation that teleological action patterns do not make up the alpha and omega of narrative art. As a matter of fact, a few decades earlier, Ortega's fellow philosopher Schopenhauer had already claimed that the eighteenth-century novel represented the "the victory of the sentient and thinking man, in particular the novel hero, over the acting man" (Zmegac 1991, 74). This collection of literary-historical observations seems to confirm my hypothesis that a new concept of time lies hidden behind the modern novel. The last few lines of Ortega's comment prove he acknowledges the character's kairos to be the main temporal dimension of modern narratives.[39]

The question remains, however, why this concept of time is not perceived as an element in an imaginal construct and why there is a wide-spread refusal to designate the temporal-spatial image associated with it. The fact is that modern texts could also be said to call up an image of the plot-space. It is certainly true that, with some exceptions, modern texts prove to be anything but plotless. If "plot" is considered to be the set of causal relationships between the events in a narrative, then this does not imply that these causal relationships ought to assume the form of a chain or linear sequence. Networks can also involve causal relationships. As indicated above, the interactions between action-space chronotopes create an image based on relationships of tension between the moments of decision the characters are going through. In this way, a network of relationships of tension between characters is created.

Lotman was one of the first to offer a typological description of this development. Pointing to the role of the mobile hero in a teleological plot-space, he argues that more complex texts necessarily require a polycentric model.

> The mobile character is split up into a paradigm-cluster of different characters on the same plane, and the obstacle (boundary), also multiplying in quantity, gives out a sub-group of personified obstacles—immobile enemy-characters fixed at particular points in the plot-space ("antagonists" to use Propp's term). (Lotman 1979, 167)[40]

Recent research shows that the plot-space in modern texts is a conglomerate of "possible worlds" (connected with the characters' cognitive operations). These worlds are what bring about the network. It is true that Homer's *Iliad* can be read from the angle of its story arc, yet it can also be read as a work of art representing prototypical relationships of tension between individuals. Even a fairly simple teleological story such as *Lazarillo de Tormes* involves some degree of psychologizing (the picaro's longing for happiness is the motor propelling the story) and a series of relationships of tension. In this sense, a clear sign is also given by modern dramatists' tendency to strip classical tragedies from their teleological "dead weight" in order to concentrate on the network of kairos moments.

It is true that many teleological stories lend themselves to a "modern" reading. At the same time, it can be said that there has been a distinct change in the course of literary history regarding the way we read. Because of narratives growing more complex, and owing to the (probably connected) preference for subjective, everyday problems, a dialogical reading increasingly became a necessity. It certainly appears to be the case that the post-Renaissance worldview, with its typical connection of time and space in modernity, has affected literary tastes. It is, there-fore, useful to take this study into a deeper analysis of the philosophical back-grounds of both types of plot-space. Choosing an interpretation in terms of either one or the other plot-space is dependent upon our readiness to accept the image of absolute time and space (which has dominated Western culture for thousands of years), or to declare it bankrupt.

SPATIALITY IN TRADITIONAL AND MODERN PLOT-SPACES

In a few essays, Bakhtin has ventured to develop a genealogy of modern mental-ity.[41] Through a series of reflections about Western narrative culture, he makes an attempt to locate a breaking point in the history of European thought which might help us to understand the different options for literary interpretation. In his view, literary history is a perfect training ground for discovering historical discontinui-ties in existing concepts of which time and space (Morson and Emerson 1990, 366; Morson 1991, 1077).

In "Epic and Novel," Bakhtin sums up a few factors that explain exactly why certain plot-space chronotopes correspond to a different worldview in a particular period. All of his arguments revolve around the fact that the novel (of Dostoevsky, among others, and of a few exceptional precursors such as Rabelais and Miguel de Cervantes) is a nonidealistic narrative form that puts a high value on imperfection and incompleteness. Premodern genres, such as the epic or the chivalric romance, are defined by Bakhtin as "complete," whereas the novel essentially is "incomplete." The fact is that completeness suggests semantic homogeneity or a fictional strat-egy to reduce the universe to basic data (eternal values and truths). This sort of worldview most often arises in cultures containing relatively stable moral codes and enabling events to continually acquire a deeper, metaphysical meaning. The creators of closed fictional worlds observe narrative events from a distance, pre-senting and interpreting everything from an Archimedean point of view.

> Thanks to this epic distance which excludes any possibility of activity and change, the epic world achieves a radical degree of completedness not only in its content but in its meaning and its values as well. The epic world is constructed in the zone of an absolute distanced image. (1981b, 7)

In modern times, new images of the fictional world are created. Heroes and hero-ines cease to be defined by an artificially closed world because the fixed moral and social codes in folkloric and urban bourgeois culture become relative. On the one hand, this evolution is expressed in certain relativistic customs that "put things in perspective" (for example, carnival). On the other hand, urban social stratification is indeed more relative than in a feudally organized countryside. In the alternative narrative tradition, heroes and heroines need to be integrated *into* history, yet without this history being determined a priori. Heroes and heroines must gain deciding authority over the course of things. As a result, the fictional world is never finished, thus acquiring a fundamentally open character.

Evidently the modern novel continues to apply older epic motifs. If these genres are imported, however, this invariably entails a new view of the semantic universe. In many picaresque stories (Miller 1967; Van Gorp 1978), for example, the element of the quest is introduced without the metaphysical undertone of the motif possessed in the chivalric romance. In Bakhtin's opinion, this concerns a tendency that is on the verge of being generalized and will be constitutive for the definition of the modern novel:

> The novel inserts into these other genres an indeterminacy, a certain seman-
> tic open-endedness, a living contact with unfinished, still evolving contem-
> porary reality (the open-ended present). (1981b, 7)

In summary, the evolution of the plot-space presented by Bakhtin in "Epic and Novel" is in keeping with the outline of the conflict chronotopes' evolution I have presented above.

The history of spatial concepts runs parallel to the developments on the level of the plot-space. In his 1967 lecture *"Des espaces autres"* ["Of Other Spaces"], Foucault's historical survey of views of spatiality in Western cultural history closely resembles Bakhtin's genealogy. Foucault argues that the Middle Ages demonstrated a tendency to arrange spaces in a hierarchical fashion. As could be expected from the eschatological perspective they expounded, the oppositions concerned the polarity of eternal, spiritual values and finite, material values. Foucault distinguishes: "sacred places and profane places, protected places and open, exposed places; urban places and rural places" (1986, 22). Because of the propensity for hierarchical arrangements, this kind of spatiality can be called a "space of emplacement." The spaces are "placed" next to, opposite to, and especially on top of each other. In his book on Rabelais, Bakhtin sketches the medieval view of spatiality in a very similar way. To a medieval person, the world is a stable space, comprised of multiple inferior, material regions, and a superior, unique region where the Divine resides (Bakhtin 1984b). In the Renaissance, this hierarchical worldview is demolished. In Bakhtin's view, Rabelais, who witnessed the bankruptcy of geocentrism and the beginning of colonial expansion, symptomatically embodies this breaking point.[42] Foucault's appraisal of the Renaissance revolution is at the same level. He argues that the concept of emplacement makes room for that of *extension*, an empirical notion of space that would be of great importance to Descartes, for example. "With Galileo and the seventeenth century," Foucault writes, "extension was substituted for localization" (1986, 23). A second revolution runs parallel to an increasing influence of bourgeois culture. Remarkably, Foucault defines the modern space of the new bourgeois world as the space of a network; it does, in fact, consist of "relations of proximity between points or elements." According to Foucault, the fact that "space takes for us the form of relations among sites" completely strips spatiality from its sacred symbolism (1986, 23).

The hypothesis of desanctification returns in Bakhtin's work, when he recognizes in Rabelais' works the symptoms of a new, uninhibited perception of spatial expansion—an expansion that takes the shape of grotesque contrasts between material elements (for example, the gigantic proportions in *Pantagruel*). More specifically, public culture in villages and cities, conjointly arranged by Bakhtin under the heading of *carnival*, nurtured Rabelais' preference for immanent forms of spatiality. Carnival offered people of the Renaissance the opportunity to develop a certain behavior that deviates from not only the customs typical for hierarchical localizations but also the regulated and normalized life required by bourgeois rationality. Carnival is a social sanctuary, a "place for working out, in a concretely sensuous, half-real and half-play acted form, a new mode of interrelationship between individuals, counterposed to the all powerful socio-hierarchical relationships of noncarnival life" (Bakhtin 1984b, 123).[43] Morson and Emerson are the only theorists who contrast Bakhtin's view of spatial expansion with both the absolutist view of space in premodern cultures and the technocratic rationality of modern life. They point out that Bakhtin transposed the contrast between Euclidean geometry (which held a monopoly for over 2,500 years) and Nikolai Lobachevsky's multidimensional geometry to the field of narrative imagination: "for Bakhtin, what is true of geometries of space is also true of chronotopes" (Morson and Emerson 1990, 368).[44] In the Rabelaisian chronotope, time and space cease to be a geometrically structured and fixed Euclidean space. They instead become a dynamic whole where time is continuously affecting the spatial constellation. For Bakhtin, Rabelais' modern concept of space is what the "space of points" is for Foucault. Both concepts seem to draw identical lessons from the Einsteinian revolution as it is related to the modern concept of space. Einstein's spacetime is (according to the glossary in Hawking and Mlodinov 2005) a "four-dimensional space of which the points are made up of events." In Einstein's view, each spatial constellation is conceived as an active, movable network that is affected by and receives its dynamics from temporal developments. In the Euclidean spatial concept, dynamics is nothing more than a geometrically describable linear (teleological) pattern. In Einstein's spacetime, it is the movement inherent to an "open" and no longer measurable or calculable network of moments in time. An expanding universe is always relative to the person observing the movement.

In a way, a dialogical view of the plot-space is as counterintuitive as Einstein's view of spacetime. After all, the teleological geometrical view of space is the one implied in our ways of dealing with space and time in everyday life. This is so, as Kermode rightly noted, because only abnormal psychological states such as

schizophrenia and intoxication are characterized by a diminished ability to antici-
pate (goal-directedness) and an increasing desire to extend the topical, existent
moment. In our normal way of dealing with time, we spatially imagine developments as geometrical "straight lines" on which qualitative leaps are situated.[45] Central to this representation is the finality of this line and its direction. The basis for
the everyday view of time is the perception of space as an absolute category, the
idea that all moments in time occur in a space that is essentially at rest. Any deviation from the postulate that space and time are absolute and basically measurable
or calculable runs counter to those commonsense perceptions. Einstein initiated a
revolution in physics when he said "that we cannot determine whether two events
having taken place at two different instances of time have occurred at the same
place in space" (Hawking and Mlodinov 2005, 38).

In narrative culture, the disappearance of an absolute measure of being at rest
implies that the dynamics of the plot-space can no longer be fixed. Therefore,
modern narrators must look for alternatives in order to render their stories dynamic. In *Narrative and Freedom* (1994, 103), Morson argues that they learned how
to apply techniques that seem to suggest they are discovering the events together
with their characters. The modern narrator does not guide his characters but now
and then enters a conversation with "characters in crisis" and by doing so gradually weaves a network of meaningful moments. He no longer looks down on a
stable world of meticulously delineated events (as is the case with a teleological
plot—the narrator looks at the events *sub specie aeternitatis*, from the perspective of
the telos); he instead infiltrates the web he personally designed.[46] Such a plot-
space—in which rhizomatic interactions between junctions occupy a central position—inevitably leads to new temporal experiences. In *The Art of Fiction*, these were
put forward by Henry James as the source of inspiration for the writer:

> What kind of experience is intended, and where does it begin and end?
> Experience is never limited and it is never complete; it is an immense sen-
> sibility, a kind of huge *spider web*, of the finest silken threads, *suspended in the
> chamber of consciousness and catching every air borne particle in its tissue*. It is the very
> atmosphere of the mind; and *when the mind is imaginative*—much more when it
> happens to be that of a man of genius—it takes to itself the faintest hints of
> life, *it converts the very pulses of the air into revelations*. (1884; my italics)

EUCLIDEAN ESCHATON AND EINSTEINIAN KAIROS

It should be abundantly clear by now that views of time simultaneously change
with views of spatiality. For example, the hierarchical, static space of the Christian
medieval world goes hand-in-hand with a preference for an eschatological concept
of time. In the eyes of the medieval, metaphysically thinking intellectual (and, for
that matter, also in the eyes of modern everyman whose metaphysical thinking

has hardly abated) time is an external feature of reality. It can be objectified, is measurable, and is essentially static.

Henri Bergson developed a sharp critique of this concept of time. He claims that in most cases the development of time is conceived as a series of discrete units (moments of time that occur in succession). Because of this, time has been spatialized and reduced to Euclidean geometry and arithmetic. The best example of this is the Aristotelian definition of a plot. Aristotle's view implies that the narrator designs a measurable timeline on which all elements are harmoniously connected with the final moment, the telos.[47] As I have said before, a metaphysical presupposition lies hidden behind this view of time and plot, that is, the idea that the goal constitutes the ultimate moment of the temporal development. For this reason, I want to connect these Euclidean views of time, especially when they are used to design a narrative plot, to the eschaton concept.

It is impossible to perfectly connect the Aristotelian concept of time, which Bergson denotes with the concept of *temps*, with the development of time in the modern novel. Anyone required to make a summary of *Crime and Punishment* will quickly note that the novel is entirely constructed around moments of crisis, moments in which a character must make a judgment (see the Greek verb *krinein*). The guilt originating from a decision propels the character and carries him or her to new moments at which judgments must again be passed (about conceding to guilt and proceeding to repentance). In this way, the character is no longer the plaything of the world he or she inhabits. Instead, the character becomes a world *sui generis*.

> The consciousness of the solitary Raskolnikov becomes a field of battle for others' voices; the event of recent days (his mother's letter, the meeting with Marmeladov), reflected in his consciousness, take on the form of a most intense dialogue with absentee participants (his sister, his mother, Sonya, and others), and in this dialogue he tries to "get his thoughts straight.". . . Raskolnikov's idea comes into contact with various manifestations of life throughout the entire novel; it is tested, verified, confirmed or repudiated by them. (Bakhtin 1984a, 88, 89)

The network of moments of crisis in the modern plot-space is in need of a new concept of time. This concept, the kairos, is based on the Bergsonian notion of duration. In the network of kairos moments, the measurable time of the clock (spatially represented as a succession of symbols representing seconds, minutes, and hours) is replaced by the temporal experience of duration.

Duration is a subjective concept of time—it belongs to the post-Kantian conception of time, which Schopenhauer called "the time in us."[48] Duration, however, represents much more than the internal concepts of time Kant worked with.

In the experience of duration, it is impossible to single out an isolated moment. All moments flow into each other and are continually joined by new impressions. Any attempt at isolating "the moment" becomes impossible.[49] The experience of duration, in other words, is a contraction of multiple moments ("elle contracte une multiplicité de moments" [Bergson 1896, 31]). Precisely because of the fact that it is a junction of moments, the experience of duration can only be defined in a relative, never in an absolute, manner. In the dentist's waiting room, time passes slowly because the duration of these moments can be compared to situations in which time seems to go much faster. The experience of duration shows itself as a relative given because a moment of experience always enters into a relationship with moments from the past. "Duration," says Deleuze, "is essentially memory, conscience, liberty. And it is conscience and liberty because it is first and foremost memory" (1968, 45).[50] Because of our uninterrupted tendency to relate a moment of experience to previous moments and the impressions these left in us, our memory is indeed the basis of our sense of time. Apart from that, the experience of duration shows us becoming conscious of (a part of) the world, and it is in this state of heightened consciousness that decisions can be made. In this sense, the moments of experiencing duration are invariably also kairos moments. In the kairos, the present is colored by the past ("it covers with a layer of memories a foundation of immediate perception" [Bergson 1896, 31]).[51] This is why the concept of kairos can be a useful tool for understanding narrative development in modern novels. A typical example of the experience of duration is the famous forty-second chapter in *The Portrait of a Lady*, in which Isabel reflects for the duration of one night about her marriage and the emotional chasm in which she finds herself. Henry James, for that matter, was very aware of the innovative nature of his philosophy of time. In the preface of a late edition of *What Maisie Knew*, James discusses a key passage in his novel ("the passage in which her father's terms of intercourse with the insinuating but so strange and unattractive lady whom he has had the detestable levity to whisk her off to see late at night"), writing that it "is a signal example of the all but incalculable way in which interest may be constituted" (1908). The kairos moment, literally and figuratively speaking, cannot be calculated.

The Bergsonian view of duration is one of the ideas about time in which the new, modern worldview is expressed. Bergson's insights are perfectly in line with the Einsteinian view of spacetime as a spatial matrix in which the points are events, yet his insights are also in keeping with older views of personal experience. Western culture did not have to wait for the modern Russian novel to assess the kairos at its true value. It also did not need Bergson to realize the importance of duration. On the contrary, the transposition of a metaphysical morality (based on supertemporal teleological processes) to the individual moral problems of modern man or woman is already present in the work of Augustine. Many innovative thinkers of the Renaissance (Luther and Jansenius, among others) relied upon Augustine's work to reform the idealistic eschatology in such a way that a new worldview came into being, possessing a realistic eschatology as its basic pattern. A new view of conflicts (and the role of human consciousness in it) was one of the most important findings of the Renaissance. Erich Frank formulates the Christian movement of renewal of the Renaissance by explicitly referring to the new approach to conflicts:

> Through the historical act of a creating will we burst through this inexorable close of nature and enter the new land of a present that determines the future. . . . Modern (wo)man also believes in the possibility of creative moments in the history of both the individual and of a people. After all, how would (s)he doubt this possibility of a free will in the self, that is to say, the power to take initiatives and consequently start a new intraworldly causal chain . . . ? Nobody seriously doubts the possibility of such creative instants in his or her own life, that is, points in time where (s)he breaks through the eternally recurring natural process and enters upon a new here and now that irredeemably renders his or her former existence past. Is the succession of these creative points in time not exactly that which we usually call "history"? (1975, 382, 390)

Augustinian views of individual consciousness are rooted in experiences of duration and kairos. In Christian modernity, truth can never be *found* inside the human being. Truth needs to be *created* by human beings. Certainly from the Renaissance onward, the human being becomes a seeker who arrives at formulating values and truths by way of personal deliberations. Just as in Augustine's *Confessions*, modern stories prefer working with heroes and heroines who aspire to "a kind of large-scale exercise in the realization of 'self-knowledge,' that is, of psychological self-integration" (De Ley 2005).[52] In our narrative culture, modern human will break open the pupal case and transform into the fledgling "problematic hero" (see Georg Lukács in *Theory of the Novel*). In the stories, a new view of humanity will be propagated, a view in which the world by definition has become an open field of possibilities.

For Bakhtin, the emergence of narratives showing the difficult personal development of an individual also constitutes a breaking or tipping point in Western narrative culture. According to him, Rabelais' work is the symptom par excellence of literature that purports to evoke the modern experience.

> Since it is a function of actual spatial and temporal growth the category of growth is one of the most basic categories in the Rabelaisian world. . . . The re-creation of a spatially and temporally adequate world able to provide a new chronotope for a new, whole and harmonious man, and for new forms of human communication. (1981a, 168)

3

Plot-Space and Morality in Western Narrative Culture

In "The Novel in Search of Itself," Pavel gives a fine outline of the options available to Western narrative culture in the sphere of morality:

> The novel raises, with extraordinary precision, the philosophical question of whether moral ideals are inherent in [humans'] world, for, if they are, why do they seem so remote from human behavior, and if they are not, why does their normative value impose itself so clearly on us? For the novel to raise this question is to ask whether, in order to defend their ideals, humans should resist the world, plunge in to try to defend moral order, or concentrate on trying to correct their own frailties. (2006, 3)

The distinction between moral ideals inherent in the world and those that lie hidden in man corresponds to the distinction between narratives that respectively evoke teleological and dialogical chronotopes. When moral ideals are inherent to the storyworld, we are dealing with external obstacles and with heroes and heroines who are the incarnations of these moral values (Grendel versus Beowulf, for example). Narratives of this kind invariably end with "the moral of the story," sometimes explicitly, sometimes implicitly. Defending the moral order and an a priori set moral objective—the eschaton—is the primary concern. Conversely, dialogical chronotopes may also contain moral ideals, yet in this case, both virtues and vices are embodied by the characters; their normative value is revealed in a conflict between mental dispositions with mental obstacles. The moral question in these narratives becomes "why should we be, and how can we be, moral?" and, "how do I correct my own weaknesses?" The plot-space in this second case notably consists of junctions where moral problems are addressed in isolation.

The contrast between these two differently integrated moral perspectives and the philosophies of time behind them constitutes this chapter's main focus. In order to clearly situate the problem, however, I will also take a look at chronotopes and narratives that do not address morality as problematic. Because mythical chronotopes contain only answers but no questions, they represent the perfect point of departure for illuminating the different way in which narratives focus attention on moral values.

Moral Negativity in Myth, Teleology, and Dialogue

As opposed to a novelistic storyworld, the universe of the myth is a world of necessity and universality. Myths comment on the world and unveil the mechanics of the world order. They emphasize the coherence between natural forces and individual gods, and they show that humanity from times immemorial—since the golden ages of the forefathers—has made itself integral to this order. Within the limits of this system, there is room for neither deviations nor anecdotal events because these do not hold stable positions in the whole. Mythical narratives concentrate on a closed space that excludes all contingency, in which everything has its place and the "outside" is very rigorously separated from the "inside." In a religiously inspired myth or in an idyll (pretty much the profane variant of a mythical pattern of thought), the negative is shut out. Danger, death, and decay are merely stages of a process that is essentially positive: from the start, danger, death, and decay represent resurrection. The judgment about the world (its development and its spatial structure) in this case bases itself on dogma or certainties. It is passed as if it were a postulate. Consequently, it can be said that myths apply a concept of time that is actually timeless: the timelessness of eternal values and truths. Time only plays a part in the form of a "repetition of the same." As a result, historical, observable processes of time are treated with much indifference: "the regularity of the repetition makes them not an anomalous and accidental occurrence, but a law immanent to the world" (Lotman 1990, 153; see also Pleij 1997). Mythical chronotopes instead show a world in which irregularity (the negative) is close to being the exception and regularity (the positive) constitutes the norm. In summary, negativity is simply ignored in myths.

It should not surprise anyone that humankind had more to tell than what was expressed in myths. Our narratives bear witness to a desire for directly confronting the negative. This confrontation derives not from a masochistic desire but stems from a longing for happiness. In his study of literary universals in epic narratives, Patrick Hogan appropriately argues that narratives are concerned with negativity because of this desire for happiness:

> Our daily lives are animated by a sense of future possibilities. We move through the seeming trivialities of ordinary existence in the hope of reaching some more encompassing goal in the longer term. In a sense the very

lack of happiness is what keeps us going. . . . Deprivation, combined with a
sense of possibility, is what gives us hope for the future. (2004, 221)

In one of the myth's variants, the idealistic eschatology, eternal values and
truths are presented by way of a narrative in which a major part is played by this
form of hope. The starting point here is a mythical state of peace and quiet ruled by
timelessness. The narrative adds temporal processes to this state, but these present
little more than a detour on the way back to the starting point. The ultimate moment, the eschaton, is the moment when things have come full circle and beginning and end become one again. The narratives we find in the mission chronotope,
identified as the first type of teleological chronotope and analyzed on the level of
the integral plot-space, apply the same temporal pattern. A mission chronotope is
nothing more than a long-drawn-out myth. As is the case with the idyll—in our
narrative culture, the example par excellence of a world-in-equilibrium—deviations
are part of the picture; however, this is only so when they serve the whole, when
decay is needed to enable growth, or when death leads to new life. In fact, the
mission chronotope *negates* negativity as much as myths do. The difference is that
it takes a longer detour. The conflict resides right in the middle of two points of
equilibrium and is seemingly annihilated by these. This detour is easily represented in spatial terms: somebody or something asks or forces the hero or heroine
to depart from home, but in the end he or she can simply return to his or her regular life.[1] During the journey, the hero or heroine does the world-in-equilibrium a
service because the regular existence of the entire world is saved through his or
her intervention.

As such, the mission chronotope actually consists of two narratives: one
about leaving home and one about returning home. In the two other variants of
teleological chronotopes, the narrative emphasis is on either the departure or the
return. In the case of the degradation chronotope, the narrative ends with a state
of homelessness (death, decay, alienation), whereas the regeneration chronotope
ends with an almost unhoped-for homecoming. The image in the regeneration
and degradation chronotope is not that of a detour but of a genuine journey, a
voyage with two components: a starting point and an end point. Each is described
in a different way, no longer as a unity—hence my mentioning a dualist concept
of time. Time is twofold: it possesses a finite component and an infinite component, an element of conflict and an element of equilibrium. In the case of the
degradation chronotope, the conflict coincides with the final point; in the other
case, the hero or heroine regenerates in the course of the narrative, and the end
is a world-in-equilibrium. Both are each other's opposite, yet both express the
same philosophy of time. In both cases, a realistic eschatology is involved: the
world of perception has as many rights as the world of eternal values and truths.
The realistic eschatology behind the degradation and regeneration chronotopes

acknowledges the negative and attempts to form a certain attitude toward it. Nevertheless, the chronotopes remain eschatological, hence, in a sense, also mythical. The final point always shows the valuable and the true: on the one hand, a world in which humans are insignificant creatures and experience trouble with establishing contact with the other elements in the world (tragic alienation); on the other hand, a world in which humans are happy to be part of a greater whole (the happy ending).

All three types of teleological chronotopes—the first to a somewhat larger extent than the other two—have something in common with the dialectical logic described by G. W. F. Hegel. In the introduction to his *Lectures on the Philosophy of History* (*Vorlesungen über die Philosophie der Geschichte*), Hegel described the perfect cycle of time: an ideal given (a principle, an ideal, a value, a valuable state of things) will manifest itself as an autotelic (purely internal) entity and subsequently externalize itself in the nonideal or the material (state of alienation in which the ideal element seems to lose itself), and return gradually to itself. In addition to this, the dialectical view of the processes of time—in this case a view of world history—entails a moral argument that recurs in teleological narratives. Hegel sees history as a theodicy or justification by God, which consists in giving evil, the morally negative, a place in a positive project. Indeed, Hegel's philosophy of time purports to reconcile "the thinking Spirit with evil."

> Indeed, nowhere is such a harmonising view more pressingly demanded than in Universal History; and it can be attained only by recognising the *positive* existence, in which that negative element is a subordinate, and vanquished nullity. On the one hand, the ultimate design of the World must be perceived; and, on the other hand, the fact that this design has been actually, realised in it, and that evil has not been able permanently to assert a competing position. (Hegel 1837)[2]

The cyclically conceived victory over negativity is perfectly expressed by the mission chronotope. It stages the mission of Hegel's "thinking Spirit" in a noncurtailed fashion. Here the negative gets totally absorbed by the affirmative, the eternal "inside" of the world order. The two other chronotopes describe two stages of the battle of the ideal and the valuable with the negative: the degradation chronotope shows how an ideal can be lost in the external world (in the "outside"), while the regeneration chronotope proves the outer world can regain itself and become "inside" again. Unlike the cyclical representation of dialectics, the resistance offered by the "outside" to the "inside" is no longer smoothed over. It is shown as an opposition. In this sense, it could be said that the idealistic eschatology acquires certain realistic features in the two latter-mentioned chronotopes.

Dialogical chronotopes can never or hardly ever be conceived as dialectical.

The plot-space called the dialogical chronotope possesses no center—there is no fixed "point of Hestia"—because the only fixed points are constituted by the values and truths that occur in the characters' mental world. For this reason, the negative can no longer be conceived as a state of the world; it is instead a given, inherent to humanity. Because the negative is never a mere feature of the outside world, it does not constitute a part of a dialectical opposition but becomes an element of a (mental) relationship of tension.[3] This is most obvious in the relationships of tension between characters. The tension between them grows as the negative in them increases.

Othello presents a perfect illustration of this dynamic because the play accumulates tension by the growing force of the negative in the title character. Evidently, the negative could be represented as if it were caught in a battle with an external obstacle (Iago), resulting in the imagining of a teleological chronotope. This representation, however, would do injustice to the subtle strategies of manipulation employed by Iago and to Othello's growing sympathy for him. The nucleus of tension resides in the increasingly intense relationship between the two characters and the influence this has on a second relationship, the one between Othello and Desdemona. There is no end goal at the heart of these relationships of tension. Furthermore, neither of these relationships of tension is at the center of the plot-space. The only central points are the rising intensity of Othello's negativity, the growing callousness of Iago, and the increasing despair of Desdemona. The central points, in other words, are taken by the negative forces and by the moments in which they are questioned—the moments of kairos. This view of negativity would be increasingly explored by Renaissance dramatists. Gradually, the novel would also become infused with a "dialogical" conception of time.

From a moral point of view, this new conception of negativity has important consequences. Within the limits of the dialogical chronotope, examples of moral values and moral role models cease to be created, even though norms are being brought up for discussion and either questioned or propagated. The modern novel stages the ways in which the norms are managed and by doing so illustrates how normality comes into being. Moretti cleverly offers convincing arguments for this hypothesis. In the modern novel, he says, two fundamental views are defended.

The first view is expressed in the *Darwinian transformation plot* (see the works of Stendhal, Aleksandr Pushkin, Balzac, and Gustave Flaubert), which offers representations of normality's problematic nature. Within the limits of this plot-space chronotope (because, in my opinion, more than merely the plot is involved), no solutions are offered for the moral negativity, and the reader is left with a feeling of "tragic" estrangement. In this case, the network of moral relationships is an open structure in which the relationships of tension are resonating just as powerfully at the end of the story as at the beginning. It is a structure in which "the survival of the fittest" represents the ultimate form of truth.

The second view defends a moral norm by highlighting a character's right moral choice. It is expressed in the *Hegelian classification plot*. In this case, we are also concerned with a network of relationships of tension, but some of these relationships actually do arrive at a final point. The classification of relationships between characters who open the narrative is demonstrably not the definitive order of the world. The fact is that some characters conquer the negative mental forces and arrive at a harmonious modus vivendi with respect to the morally negative.[4] These characters have access to ideals of normality, representations of the good life or of the desirable communal life. As opposed to the morality highlighted in teleological narratives, the propagated idea of "normality" is not a postulate. The moral truth in the dialogical chronotope is gradually unveiled. The narrative demonstrates how the characters, step by step, from kairos to kairos, draw nearer to a form of self-knowledge and insight into their own motives. The narrative does not advance values or truths, but it does uncover them by staging the characters' supreme mental efforts.[5]

Mythical Versus Narrative Chronotopes

TIMELESS REGULARITY: TIME IN SACRED MYTHS

In the preceding chapter, I associated myths with the idyllic passages, often encountered in narratives (examples are the harmonious opening and end situations of an adventure story). Idyllic passages were introduced as the "profane" variants of mythical thought because by a perfect, regular equilibrium chronotope, they expressed the shared existence of human beings and the relationship between man and nature. The purely mythical chronotope takes this one step further: the myth presents an equilibrium chronotope composed of abstract values and principles, even though hardly any dynamism is injected into the storyline. In sacred myths, regularity is not merely an object of description; it is also represented as sacred and inviolable. The ambition of myths is to present the building blocks of the world as a coherent system.

In myths, the mythical poet and the audience submit themselves to the timeless truth of eternal cosmic processes. They engage themselves in superindividual processes, thereby permitting time to free itself from individual experiences. Idylls are invariably predisposed to sacralize collective traditions and interactions with nature by isolating the regularity in society and nature and elevating it to a structure that is independent of individual action. Myths follow through on this inclination. The described phenomena become universal truths. Because of this, myths also establish universal norms (murder, vengeance, and malediction are demonized and ascribed to timeless divine powers), a function at which they prove to be very successful. The sacred character of myths was secured by the mere fact that they were timelessly recounted in oral narrative culture. For centuries, they served as a body of stories that were traditionally handed down and confirmed the value of the accepted truths. Friedrich Nietzsche, in *Menschliches, Allzumenschliches (Human, All Too Human)*, was well aware of the fact that traditions are formidable tools for establishing social cohesion:

> Now, each tradition grows more venerable the farther its origin lies in the past, the more it is forgotten; the respect paid to the tradition accumulates from generation to generation; finally the origin becomes sacred and awakens awe; and thus the morality of piety is in any case much older than that morality which requires selfless acts. (1878, par. 96)

In contrast to idylls, myths do more than simply pay tribute to repeatable traditions in a universe that moves forward in a cyclical manner. In the myths of gods and ancestors, for example, the influence of norm-establishing traditions reaches its zenith.[6] It is actually not tradition that is staged in these stories, but the *origin* of tradition. In this sense, these narratives constitute the best examples of sacred myths. The Africanist Mineke Schipper observes, "Myths explain the origin of man, his relationships with the gods, the forefathers, the land on which he lives, the surrounding nature and his own culture. Also described in myths is the world of gods and the lives of the primordial forefathers" (1999, 9). At first sight, these myths strongly resemble idylls: a community of gods is a family who meets regularly (for example, at feasts at Asgard and Mount Olympus) and operates in an enclosed and well-defined space (Asgard as a walled empire of the gods, the unattainable Mount Olympus), and in which every member fulfills a specific function. Myths about gods and forefathers take this one step further than idylls because they claim to describe an original well-balanced state. In *The Philosophy of Symbolic Forms*, Cassirer explains that the essence of mythological thought is found in a temporal and spatial logic that differs radically from the logic of other worldviews. The sanctification of an original temporal and spatial state is of crucial importance for myth.[7] On the one hand, myths introduce—on the spatial level—a sharp distinction between an inside world that encloses the sacred original forces and an outside world consisting of empirical, fleeting events. Mythical thought expresses the conviction that eternal forces govern the cosmos and that those forces have a spatial foundation; it believes that the seemingly chaotic forces of nature have a stable center and preserve their harmonious rhythm from here to eternity.

> Every mythically significant content, every circumstance of life that is raised out of the sphere of the indifferent and commonplace, forms its own ring of existence, a walled-in zone separated from its surroundings by fixed limits. (Cassirer 1975, 103)

On the other hand, the predilection for an original state also leaves its marks on the conception of time. Indeed, history will be *annulled* in sacred myths because their explanation of the world implies always a link "with a unique event in the past, which discloses its mythical generation" (Cassirer 1975, 105).

> Time does not take the form of a mere relation, in which the factors of present, past, and future are persistently shifting and interchanging; here, on the contrary, a rigid barrier divides the empirical present from the mythical origin and gives to each its own inalienable "character". Thus it is understandable that the mythical consciousness . . . has sometimes been called a timeless consciousness. For compared with objective time, whether cosmic or historical, mythical time is indeed timeless. (Cassirer 1975, 106)

Myths stage an attempt to return (or, at the very least, look back) to an original era, hoping that humanity can relive the past in the here and now. Cosmogonies, for example, describe the cosmos in its original state and demonstrate how the deity or the team of gods proceeds to create a world. In telling a creational story, a narrator wants to impart something about not only the creation of the cosmos but also the regularity in the actual, natural world. The creation is the beginning of a repetitive creational process in which the cycle of nature (seasons, birth of new generations) is featured for the first, but not for the last, time. Like any other sacred myth, a creational myth tells about the origin of an ontological order. It tells about a stable system that has not only possessed a certain structure from its origin but also, since then, has preserved this structure and will continue to do so for eternity.

The difference with the more profane idylls lies in the fact that the processes portrayed in them are situated outside of human time. Sometimes, a profane conception of time is used along with a representation of sacred time. The following text demonstrates that profane idyllic representations are among the basic ingredients of the sacred myth in the Judeo-Christian world. Ecclesiastes, chapter 3, shows that regular patterns from collective and biological life are used to confirm the universality of the universe:

> *To every thing there is a season, and a time to every purpose under the heaven: A time to be born, and a time to die;* a time to plant, and a time to pluck up that which is planted; A time to kill, and a time to heal; a time to break down, and a time to build up; A time to weep, and a time to laugh; a time to mourn, and a time to dance; A time to cast away stones, and a time to gather stones together; a time to embrace, and a time to refrain from embracing; . . . What profit hath he that worketh in that wherein he laboureth? I have seen the travail, which God hath given to the sons of men to be exercised in it. *He hath made every*

thing beautiful in his time: also he hath set the world in their heart (King James Bible, Ecclesiastes 3:1–5, 9–11; my italics)

In these biblical verses, idyllic regularity is attributed to God, a common religious operation. Although the cyclical processes are initially described as immanent phenomena, the subsequent verses point at a supertemporal character:

He hath made every thing beautiful in his time: also he hath set the world in their heart, *so that no man can find out the work that God maketh from the beginning to the end.* I know that there is no good in them, but for a man to rejoice, and to do good in his life. [13] And also that every man should eat and drink, and enjoy the good of all his labour, it is the gift of God. I know that, *whatsoever God doeth, it shall be for ever:* nothing can be put to it, nor any thing taken from it: and God doeth it, that men should fear before him. *That which hath been is now; and that which is to be hath already been;* and God requireth that which is past. (King James Bible, Ecclesiastes 3:11–15; my italics)

Profane myths differ from sacred myths because in the latter the world is described as a timeless unit. Sacred myths confirm the continuity between origin and present: the cosmos continues to work as it had once worked in the beginning. The origin featured in the story is one that works proactively: the forces that were present then still play a leading role today. The audience that attached and attaches great importance to myths makes the assumption that the original continues to exist into the present and that it will live on for ever and ever. In this way, for mythical man, a world emerges that resembles the fate-obsessed society Jorge Luis Borges described in "La lotería en Babilonia" (The Babylon Lottery) (1941). At first, this lottery, in which nearly everyone participated (making those who do not play look despicable), merely consisted of hoping to obtain a winning ticket, which yielded considerable amounts of money. After a decline in interest for the game, unlucky tickets were introduced. Despite that fact that drawing an unlucky ticket could result in death, the lottery regained its popularity. Like the Babylonians in Borges, mythical cultures feel a strong connection with fate (the fact that the Babylonians are the fathers of astrology undoubtedly played its part in the choice of the story's location). In myths, submission to the necessity and irreversibility of fate drowns out the idyllic fascination for nature's rhythm and can sometimes lead to very strict rituals. Instead of describing nature's regularity from the perspective of human labor, myths of fertility, for example (see Frazer's description of the forest king myth in *The Golden Bough*), resort to allegory: they ignore the role of man or woman and evoke nature's rhythm as the death and resurrection of a fertility god.

RITUALS

Rituals are another cultural strategy that deals with the morally negative. Myths put humans out of action, as in Frazer's myths of fertility. Rituals, on the contrary, are intended to bring humanity into contact with the mythical world. For humans to share in this world, they must perform actions that can conjure up favors from the mythical world's inhabitants. Rituals, unlike myths, represent strategies for dealing with the negative. A myth, for example, would state that a fertility king has died and that a new king will rise from his ashes. In a ritual, the statement of myth is substituted with the action of a mortal man burning part of his fruits (the crop of his land) in offerings, hoping that the gods will grant him renewed fertility in exchange. In some ethnic groups, the beginning of spring is marked by a ceremony which involves a cake with a bean hidden inside; the poor wretch who finds the bean in his or her piece of the cake is cast into a fire to exact fertility from the gods.

In the ritual, humanity enters the eternal world of the myth. In fact, the myth stages a homecoming: a man or woman abandons his or her limited worldly existence (conceived as an "outside") and regains home in the world of eternal values (the "inside"). Rituals deal with Tyche and Hermes. They are a homecoming in the perfect world of Aion and Hestia, who are the center of the worldview. The other two, as Vernant put it, are merely mobile intermediaries, the detours. The ritual homecoming occurs in three forms that show strong resemblances with the above-mentioned teleologically structured chronotopes.

1. The ritual of sacrifice (as found in the fertility rituals so dear to James Frazer and T. S. Eliot): a person sacrifices him- or herself, dies (or *performs* the act of "ceasing to exist" by offering a share of his or her crop) then regains life (the good—renewed fertility—is his or her reward). These fertility rituals manifest a perfect dialectical circle: the point of departure is positive, the intermediary stage is negative, but the final point constitutes a return to the positive.
2. The ritual of punishment (in the Durkheimian sense, see Garland 1990, 9): a person, either forcibly or not, submits him- or herself to pain and is banned from the mythical world. Flagellation becomes the symbol of being cast into or chained to the realm of the senses. This is also the ritual of demotion in a military context (the removal of all honorary signs that indicate a high-ranking military position).
3. The ritual of initiation (as described for instance by Arnold Van Gennep in 1909): at first, the person resides in a closed space and is lifted to a higher level of truth. In many rites of passage or initiation, the novice is initially left to die but is subsequently recovered and then reaccepted in the community under a new identity. A closed space (symbolized by

a pit or a grave) is forced open to allow the initiated to breathe freely again in an open, free space. The ritual of baptism shows the same logical pattern (symbolically drowning in the water, then emerging from it).

These three expressions of ritual behavior neatly correspond to the three ways in which teleological narratives deal with negativity. The worldly eschatology strongly resembles the last two strategies, the circular idealistic eschatology the first.

1. A mission chronotope follows the same circular logic as the ritual of fertility. The hero or heroine sacrifices him- or herself, a part of him- or herself, or a subordinate in order to restore the world's equilibrium. For this purpose, the hero or heroine must cross the boundary of the negative if he or she is to enter the world of adventure (the conflict chronotopes). During the final moment, the hero or heroine and his or her community celebrate the (actual, but invariably also metaphorical) homecoming.[8]

2. A degradation chronotope ends with the exclusion of the hero or heroine from his or her home world. The negative is not caught between two moments of balance, but constitutes the narrative's apotheosis. Of the circle of departure-adventure-return, only the part of "departure" is left in this chronotope. Hence, in classical tragedy, the punishment of the hero or heroine will be the moral message's supporting surface.

3. In a regeneration chronotope, the conflict chronotope is situated at the beginning of the narrative; it gives the initial impetus to a process of rehabilitation or reform that ends with the confirmation of values and truth. The character ends up in a degenerated situation or state and, during the entire course of the narrative, hopes that this degeneration will be followed by a regeneration. The process here can be compared to a conversion: the hero or heroine reverses his or her moral attitude and thereby changes his or her fate. Of the circle of departure-adventure-return, only the part of the return is left in this chronotope. The prototypes here are the horror story and the love story or romance.[9]

MYTH AND ESCHATOLOGY

The ritual is an important intermediary in understanding the transition from mythical to purely narrative chronotopes. Another cultural phenomenon that may clarify the same transition is the eschatological narrative—neither the theory nor the philosophy of time, but the narrative, as such, in the sense of the story Christians tell about Christ. The difference between these types of religious narratives and the mythical representations of the sacred is that the first integrate the accidental and submit it to the laws of sacral intentionality. By contrast, mythical narratives have a condescending attitude toward contingent experiences and have no need for intentional or goal-directed processes. In this respect, the myth confirms what Nietzsche said when he linked the idea of purpose with the notion of accident in *Die fröhliche Wissenschaft* (*The Gay Science*): "Once you know that there are no purposes, you also know that there is no accident; for it is only beside a world of purposes that the word 'accident' has meaning" (2001: 109). Myths are ignorant of individual intentional, goal-directed behavior and therefore also eliminate accident and contingency—exactly what narratives require for an interplay of concepts of time to manifest themselves.

Nevertheless, narrative culture has found a solution for the seemingly impossible combination of mythical self-sufficiency and regularity, on the one hand, and human objectives and accidental events, on the other hand. This solution, Lotman says, was found in the form of the eschatological narrative pattern. Indeed, in order to include external deviations into the narrative and to make danger and turmoil a subject of discussion, a new type of storytelling was created. Eschatological narratives reconcile the two types of time introduced in the previous chapter: the universal-necessary time, that is, the timeless regularity of the closed system (the chronotope of equilibrium); and the particular-contingent time, the time of man and of which man is the measure (the chronotope of conflict). Apart from granting considerable space to truths about universal laws, eschatological narratives also find room for man and his history. It goes without saying that these narratives, which essentially employ the same components as the nonreligious teleological narratives, represent the most vital link in the genealogical reconstruction of moralism in teleological narrative art. The moralizing tendency of mythical narratives links itself to history, that is, to a succession of actions that are part of the human world of experience.

A Typology of Teleological Chronotopes

The combination of eternity and history makes eschatology an important mediator in narrative culture. It designates the transition from a religious-dogmatic culture to a historicizing culture. It is in this culture that a space will be kept for the narrative chronotopes that were outlined above by means of ritual types. Narratives, when read from an eschatological logic, are linearized versions of a mythical system in which the timeless order is assigned a place on a storyline of chaos and contingencies. It is no accident that chronotopes of mission, degradation, and regeneration are related to religious eschatologies. They share the same philosophy of time and employ the same preference for teleological plot-space chronotopes.

These narrative chronotopes stop proclaiming dogmas about humanity, the world, and the divine. Instead, they propagate quests for existential truths.

> By creating plot-texts humanity learnt to distinguish plots in life and in this way to make sense of life. (Lotman 1990, 170)

TRIUMPHANT MORALITY IN THE MISSION CHRONOTOPE

A mission chronotope owes its name to the boundary-breaking mission heroes and heroines must accomplish in adventure stories. Campbell's *The Hero with a Thousand Faces* (first published in 1949) contains a schema (Campbell 1968, 245) that nicely summarizes the circular, dialectical movement of the mission chronotope and, in addition, highlights the boundary that will be broken. The circle describes an initial movement from an opening situation over to a "call to adventure," to an apotheosis (a sacred marriage, a father atonement, an elixir theft) and is closed by a flight movement that consists in fact of a return to the initial state. Both movements are characterized by a crossing of a border, a crossing of "the threshold of adventure" (in the first movement, this could be, for instance, a battle with a dragon, and in the second movement, the rescue of the hero, a resurrection, or a threshold struggle). In an implicit comment on this schema, Lotman (1979) writes that the world of adventure is a split world. It is a world in which an "inside" is confronted with an "outside," or, in the terminology of this book, a world in which images of equilibrium contrast with images of conflict. On the one hand, the plot-space contains without exception a representation of an equilibrium chronotope, an image expressing moral, emotional, or truth-related judgments. On the other hand, it contains a conflict chronotope where great strain is put on these kinds of ideals. In the equilibrium chronotope, the hero or heroine experiences a call to deliver a contribution to the conservation of these ideals (a "call to adventure" from a superior commanding force). Additionally, a morally high-ranking character promises the hero or heroine support. This equilibrium chronotope possesses fragile ideals that must be rehabilitated over and over again. It, therefore, craves an "elixir" that will guarantee its vitality. In the conflict chronotope, the hero or heroine's moral, emotional, and cognitive commitment is put to the test. He or she receives the promised help (for instance, through a magical gift from the equilibrium chronotope) but must make regretful sacrifices (a peace offering by the father figure) and will seem to be overcome with danger (flight).[10]

Campbell's view is little more than a rewrite of Propp's *Morphology of the Folktale* from the 1920s. Nevertheless, his analysis has the advantage of fixating less on the plot's progress (as in Propp's succession of thirty-one functions) and focusing more on the plot-space. Just as in Greimas' actantial schema (Keunen 2005, 165–83), the narrative is represented by Campbell as an integral space. As a result, the rhythm of change between conflict and equilibrium becomes the center of attention, allowing an analysis from the perspective of genre theory (a typological comparison). Conflict and equilibrium receive a specific meaning in the mission chronotope. Although I have already discussed many elements of conflict and equilibrium chronotopes, I would like to briefly explain again how action-space chronotopes acquire their moral meaning.

Morality and Conflict in Mission Stories

The conflict chronotope can be summarized in one word by the concept of *boundary*. The boundary that separates the equilibrium chronotope from the conflict chronotope must be crossed twice: a first time when stepping out of the positive world, a second time when returning to it. This boundary, however, is not only the dividing line between a familiar and an alien space; it also takes the symbolic shape of a series of obstacles. The obstacles at issue are hostile to (or sometimes even a downright reversal of) the internal space: a monster that preys on the community, a devious knight or brother, an abduction, a difficult physical situation such as a tempest or an extreme physical exertion, and so on. These types of symbolic boundaries present themselves multiple times in one single narrative. The boundary breaking is repeated several times in different episodes: a first victory, for instance, will turn out to be only a temporary and apparent breaking of the boundary; it is repeated in a second and third victory (see *Beowulf*). During the return, the boundary is expressed in new symbolic obstacles: an accidental rescue from the negative world, a successful homecoming with the found or regained object, a favorable end to a physical emergency situation, to name but a few examples.

In other words, the plot-space of a mission chronotope consist of a series of morally charged contingent events (conflict chronotopes) that are attributed to persons, objects, and situations and help forward or obstruct the hero's actions. The most evident examples of this process are found in the superhero story, a famous example of twentieth-century American popular culture (featuring heroes such as Superman, Spider-Man, and Batman, as well as action thrillers featuring Arnold Schwarzenegger, Sylvester Stallone, or Jean-Claude Van Damme) and in adventure tales (*The Frog-King, or Iron Henry; The Tin Soldier; Snow-White and Rose-Red; The Brave Little Tailor*). In an ironic commentary, Brian Attebery describes the stereotyped form of conflict chronotopes by means of Tolkienesque fantasy stories:

> Take a vaguely medieval world. Add a problem, something more or less ecological, and a prophecy for solving it. Introduce one villain with no particular characteristics except a nearly all-powerful badness. Give him or her a convenient blind spot. Pour in enough mythological creatures and non-human races to fill out a number of secondary episodes: fighting a dragon, riding a winged horse, stopping overnight with the elves (who really should

organize themselves into a bed-and-breakfast association). To the above mixture add one naive and ordinary hero who will prove to be the prophesied savior; give him a comic sidekick and a wise old advisor who can rescue him from time to time and explain the plot. Keep stirring until the whole thing congeals. (1992, 10)

Morality and Equilibrium in Mission Stories

In the mission chronotope, the equilibrium chronotope receives less attention than the conflict chronotope but nevertheless serves as the moral cornerstone of the narrative. In a narrative of this sort, the equilibrium chronotope represents the mythical element and the eschaton. In harmony with the eschatological roots of the mission chronotope, however, the myth will often be integrated in a more worldly form, that is, in the form of an idyll.[11] The idyll is perhaps the most important expression of the equilibrium chronotope in mission narratives.

A first characteristic that dominates the staging of an idyllic state of equilibrium is the representation of fictional space as an isolated space and a closed system. In the traditional idyll, this may refer to the secluded locales resembling the Arcadia of Hercules, the enclosed valley in the Peloponnesian peninsula that constitutes an oasis in a barren landscape. Nothing much is changed in later idyllic representations: preferred are the harmonious settings of a farming community (a village by a river in a valley; a farmyard with land, barns, and a house; a pastoral environment providing opportunities for pleasure); a familiar mountain range encompassing a valley; a river, still running through the residential area after many centuries; and so on. Enduring elements in the landscape are strongly accentuated. Idyllic situations typically exhibit a sharp partitioning of the familiar and the alien. The closed system seems surrounded by an unknown, uninteresting, or frightening alienness. A perfect description of a closed system is contained in the prologue of *The Lord of the Rings* in which J. R. R. Tolkien provides an outline of the history, geography, and cultural habits of the Shire. Additionally, the opening scene of the first book (the arrival of Gandalf in Hobbiton and the festival celebrating Bilbo's birthday) offers a concrete manifestation of this closed culture. The fact is that idyllic spaces appear in many popular genres. The long-drawn-out love story in bestselling melodramas in the fashion of Judith Krantz, Harold Robbins, Jackie Collins, Heinz Konsalik, or Hedwig Courths-Mahler employs (intermediary) equilibriums of tension of the idyllic type even more than the concise Mills and Boon type of romance.

A second moral feature of the equilibrium chronotope concerns the characters' behavior (the temporal dimension), resulting from the mythical space's dimension of Hestia. A symptomatic example is the closing sentence of many fairytales: "they married and lived happily ever after." The expression emphasizes that the hero or heroine allows him- or herself to be integrated into a larger whole. In mission chronotopes, this emphasis invariably recurs. They nearly always suggest a feeling of community or evoke equilibrium between man and nature. Marriages or engagements belong to the standard situations that represent the beginning and/or the end. Adventure tales (*The Bee Queen, The Brave Little Tailor*) and the Greek adventure romance provide the finest examples, but epics, too, frequently resort to idyllic representations. Funerals or deaths structure the beginning and end of *Beowulf* and *The Aeneid*, while pastoral harmony often forms the idyllic operating base of generation and regional novels. In the representation of communal life, heroes and heroines confirm the harmonious repetition that characterizes the world: collective labor (interaction with nature: sowing, harvesting, resowing a part of the harvest), reproduction (choosing a partner, birth, education, choosing a new partner, and so on), and ritual festivities (harvesting, initiation, marriage, birth; see also Vlasov 1995, 43) constitute points of anchorage in the construction of narratives. As Norbert Elias (1985, 27) has shown, these collective activities confirm nature's rhythm, repeating the life cycles of the physical and biological world. Even when the ties with natural cycles are loosened in later periods of Western civilization, the collective celebration of regularity retained its importance. To this day, stories illustrate the ways in which people form alliances to engage in a fight against nature (consider disaster movies) and set up partnerships in small or medium-sized communities such as those found in soap operas. Because of this, physical or biological nature appears as the norm of temporal development:

> Human life and nature are perceived in the same categories. The seasons of the year, ages, nights and days . . . , copulation (marriage), pregnancy, ripening, old age and death: all these categorial images serve equally well to plot the course of an individual life and the life of nature (in its agricultural aspect). (Bakhtin 1981a, 209)

In this respect, it should be noted that Bakhtin refers to this cyclical conception as "the folkloric time." Indeed, this imaginal representation of temporal patterns strongly resembles traditional situations that deviate from modernity. In keeping with the discussions raging in the Proletcult movement, he connects the human predilection for cyclical processes of time with an ancient, precapitalist stage in Western culture and in this way emphasizes the collective nature of human life. Following Maxim Gorki and Anatoli Lunacharski, Bakhtin perceives folk culture as a culture where collectivity had not yet become an idle concept (Simons 1996, 129–51). In this culture, people devote their attention to what he calls "the old matrix" (Bakhtin 1981a, 230), a set of practices (love, birth, death, marriage, work, eating and drinking, stages of growth; Bakhtin 1981a, 225–26) that were the object of a collective experience and were structured—here he differs from Gorki— by a folkloric concept of time.

The three previously mentioned moral features—collective labor, reproduction, and ritual festivities—all revolve around collectivity and regularity. In this sense, the genre appears to favor sociobiology or evolutionary psychology, which holds that the human herd instinct is shaped by evolutionary processes acting through our genes (see Wilson 1978). Evidently, one does not need to be a sociobiologist to acknowledge that collectivity is a crucial aspect of human existence and a basic dimension of the human life story. At the other end of the philosophical spectrum, in phenomenology or existentialist philosophy (which highlight the free, autonomous project of life, more or less the antithesis of a sociobiological interpretation of collectivity), collectivity is viewed as a basic condition of human existence. Heidegger, for example, does not simply regard *Mitsein* as an accidental ontic given but, on the contrary, considers it to be an ontological existential, a fundamental condition of possibility for the human *Dasein*. In a recent commentary on Heidegger, Jean-Luc Nancy and Laurens Ten Kate summarize this argument as follows:

> We must think the community as a "groundform" and not a side-effect of human existence. As soon as people are exposed to one another in a plurality—and what else could humanity be than precisely this reciprocal exposition of people and peoples?—"there is community." But this fundamental form of community is not simply their product, nor their operation or "oeuvre"; it is not just the sum of individuals *having* something in common. It is a place where they, inadvertently, *are* in common, only to discover that this "in-common" cannot be controlled by them and so eludes them. (2004)

These kinds of reflections profoundly illuminate the mission chronotope. From the narrative perspective of the profane (or secular) myth, only the collective aspects of human experience are brought up. Exceptional or abnormal incidents are irrelevant and manifest themselves only when the story tends toward adventurous, anecdotal, or tragic events that flourish in the actual stories. In the mission chronotope, the passing of time is stripped of all contingency. Life cycles are oblivious to decay because death and dying are but secondary moments within a process of growth, blooming, bearing fruit, ripening, and expanding. Regularity is the central given; the narrative revolves not only around the return of regularity at the end of the narrative but also in the intermediary short-lived representations of harmony. Therefore, the expectation of equilibrium is what is substantial because within the story arc it serves as the thread that confers order on the events. The narrative seems to implicitly state that equilibrium and harmony are necessary and inevitable. The anecdotal, the adventurous, and the contingent may occur with equal (or even greater) frequency, but they are merely accidental, seemingly arising from the substantial equilibrium or posing an external threat to it. They are never a necessity and will in the course of the narrative (and certainly at the end) turn out to be contingent side effects in a world of regularity. The adventure in these narratives presents itself as the "collateral damage," which does not essentially affect the order of things.

The Moral Victory March of the Mission's Hero

It is striking that in the mission chronotope secondary characters are reduced to being elements of the conflict chronotope. As I have said in the first section of this chapter, secondary characters belong to the spatial background or setting. All attention goes to the character who performs the boundary-breaking and undergoes the rhythm of exodus and return. Propp is right to call this character the "hero-as-a-seeker" because his or her quest for the eschaton carries the dynamics and is the basis of every change.[12] In the folktales Propp examined, as well as in texts by the Brothers Grimm and Charles Perrault, the hero or heroine is charged with a moral task by a (frequently older and wiser) commanding character. This task consists of encountering (and beating) immoral opponents and finding a particular lost or stolen object in order to return it to the rightful community. In other quest narratives, the hero or heroine seeks a desired person (Penelope in the *Odyssey*, Guinevere in *Lancelot, or, the Knight of the Cart*, Princess Leia in *Star Wars*) or, in more recent times, a killer (the classic crime story). In a mission chronotope, the hero or heroine confronts the threat or begins the quest for the object that is stolen from the community; the missing object can be tangible, such as a princess, or intangible: peace, truth, or justice. The moral ethos of the hero or heroine is set on bringing order to chaos in a given situation. He or she realizes the absence of the community's laws in particular. Therefore, this ethos can be called a *nomothetic* ethos—the hero or heroine behaves as a lawmaker. This is amply demonstrated by the dialogue between M and James Bond that sets off the action in Ian Fleming's *For Your Eyes Only*:

> There were no doubts in Bond's mind. He didn't know the Havelocks or care who they were. Hammerstein had operated the law of the jungle on two defenceless old people. Since no other law was available, the law of the jungle should be visited upon Hammerstein. In no other way could justice be done. If it was revenge, it was the revenge of the community. Bond said: "I wouldn't hesitate for a minute, sir. If foreign gangsters find they can get away with this kind of thing they'll decide the English are as soft as some other people seem to think we are. This is a case for rough justice—an eye for an eye." (1960, 70)

The seeker-hero is a character perceived by the recipient to be fundamentally different from ordinary mortals and thus from the recipient him- or herself.[13] This does not, however, prevent him from feeling connected with the hero or heroine on a moral level. Sherlock Holmes's genius, Superman's supernatural power, Lancelot's bravery, and James Bond's composure have become legendary without anyone ever having the nerve to criticize them for their superhuman qualities. The audience empathizes with heroic capabilities, whatever their hyperbolic magnification, and enjoys the hero's or heroine's flair in overcoming obstacles. This fondness for perfect heroes and heroines is an extension of what I have previously identified as the desire for balance and harmony, for an equilibrium. Thanks to his or her exceptional qualities, a real hero or heroine succeeds in realizing the regularity inherent in the turbulent world of adventure. His or her behavior is an interrupted continuation of harmonious regularity. He or she may be an exaggeration of perfection, yet this is not in the least perceived to be disturbing: what matters is that the character oozes confidence, just as the state of equilibrium at the beginning of the narrative does. The hero or heroine is an imperturbable lawmaker, an untouchable nomothete. Amid all the turmoil arising from breaching the equilibrium, the hero or heroine continues to stolidly testify to the fact that regularity rules the world, hence his or her imperturbability (which is in fact a fine symbol of all his or her superior qualities). Whatever the culture in which he or she appears, the hero or heroine of the mission chronotope always and everywhere pledges regularity. This was already apparent from Lancelot's behavior, which I have mentioned before (see chapter 2, "A Typology of Conflict Chronotopes: Tyche and Hermes"). Centuries later, the moral symbolism of imperturbable heroes and heroines has not lost a shred of its attraction:

> The explosions from the Colt .45 were deafening. The two birds disintegrated against the violet backdrop of the dusk, the scraps of feathers and pink flesh blasting out of the yellow light of the café into the limbo of the deserted street like shrapnel. There was a moment of deafening silence. James Bond didn't move. He sat where he was, waiting for the tension of the deed to relax. It didn't. With an inarticulate scream that was half a filthy word, Tiffy took James Bond's bottle of Red Stripe off the counter and clumsily flung it. There came a distant crash of glass from the back of the room. Then, having made her puny gesture, Tiffy fell to her knees behind the counter and went into sobbing hysterics. James Bond drank down the rest of his beer and got slowly to his feet. (Fleming 1965, 62)

By means of their superhuman qualities, seeker-heroes such as James Bond neutralize the element of chance dominating the conflict chronotope. Consequently, they can be called *guardians of the (mythical) law*, while their actions can be labeled as sacred. In accordance with the values that guarantee his or her community a regular existence (and probably for that exact reason), the hero or heroine possesses an inviolability that precludes even the slightest accessibility because he or she forces spectators and readers into a distanced contemplation.[14] A hero or heroine possessing moral charisma must be immune to the contingencies that befall him or her during the mission, but, more importantly, he or she must also be immune to the contingencies of human existence itself.

PUNISHMENT IN THE DEGRADATION CHRONOTOPE
Morality and Equilibrium for Tragic Heroes and Heroines

Sacred heroes and heroines are also prominently featured in tragic narratives such as those conceived by Sophocles. They personify the community's laws or the "heart" of the community as well as symbolizing regularity and order, in the sense that they represent perfect kings, exemplary mothers, and ideal warriors. Their ethos is that of collectivity, of the sense of "we" and "us." This is beautifully demonstrated in a key passage from the first act of *Oedipus Rex*: the hero, carrying great prestige because he defeated the sphinx, proposes to his people that he will lead them through the desert and free them from the plague. Oedipus is cunning (he subdues the sphinx), brave (he kills a tyrant who, of course, turns out to be his father), compassionate (he wants to free Thebes from the plague), sincere (he is consistent in his pursuit of the truth), and filled with a sense of responsibility. Nevertheless, he suffers a tragic outcome. His status of being untouchable gives way to an image of someone whose actions are completely heterotelic. As it turns out, this particular hero's mission does *not* lead to his homecoming and the community. Moreover, the character degrades from a hero to an insignificant human being. From a world that fully enclosed the hero and offered him a home, the fictional world deteriorates into a closed world of which the hero can or may no longer be part.

True, the hero's demise is the final point in this teleological chronotope, but is it by no means the narrative's eschaton. An eschaton only becomes a moral end when Hestia and Aion are confirmed. In the tragedy, the morality behind the hero's or heroine's life always possesses another side, which is rightfully called the real eschaton. This other side of morality becomes visible when the religious-moral dimension of the degradation chronotope is taken into account. From the perspective of the gods, the initial situation is far from harmonious. The so-called sacred hero or heroine serves as a pattern of unwarranted behavior and undesirable situations. Oedipus is guilty of a moral mistake, a defect typical for humanity: hubris. When the oracle predicts that Oedipus will do something that runs counter to his sense of value and to the community's values, the hero refuses to acquiesce. He leaves and believes he can undo the prophecy of the oracle. Every religious human being knows this to be nonsense. A prophecy from the gods is binding, and only the vain believe that man is without error. Indeed, only a vain hero such as

Oedipus could think that he had found the perfect way out and has succeeded in taking his life back into his own hands again.

From Oedipus's perspective the tragic ending may be heterotelic, but from the perspective of the gods the Eschaton is indeed attained. We could even go as far as saying that Oedipus's story contains a regeneration chronotope: the sinful world is transformed into a harmonious world, characterized by eternal values and truths. The end point of the narrative is the demise of the amoral hero or heroine and the victory of mythical perfection. However, the label of "regeneration" would not be justified. The fact remains that the action-space in a tragedy is not dominated by gods but by human beings. It is the tragic hero or heroine who rules the action-space, and it is his or her actions that will guide the reading. Therefore, the telos can neither be ascribed to the hero's or heroine's demise nor be located in the divine triumph. In this case, the telos is instead found in the idea of punishment. It is punishment that shows the ultimate conflict between superior and inferior values. It shows a conflict chronotope paradoxically bringing up the eschaton: the hero's or heroine's demise (his or her heterotelic behavior) and the gods' eschaton are harmoniously united in the punishment. It is no coincidence that Aristotle called the effect of this harmonious final point "the catharsis." The punishment ends in the repentance of hero or heroine and audience. The act of moral cleansing draws to a close when the hero or heroine undergoes rightful punishment. The repentance of both hero or heroine and audience heralds the return of the equilibrium.[15]

Morality and Conflict in Tragic Stories

In the same way as the idyll forms a basic pattern for representing regularity and harmony, so an old genre can be said to offer the most complete imaginal representation of chance and contingency in the degradation chronotope: the elegy. Lamentations of death and misfortune, as well as metaphysical reflections on mortality, constitute the nucleus of narrative art. As Frye correctly argued, however, they appear to shine brightest in the narratives of tragic heroes and heroines offered by the history of literature (1973, 43). The elegiac refers to a narrative component present in all narratives: the threat of imminent failure and the confrontation with the acting character's demise.[16] Elegiac grief is entirely concerned with the failure of problem-solving abilities. Conversely, it can be said that the successful solving of a problem elicits euphoria and happiness. In both cases, narrative art tells us something about a fundamentally human experiential invariable. The dysphoria and euphoria we experience when empathizing with narrative heroes and heroines shows humanity in the pursuit of self-preservation. The frustration spawned by the confrontation with chance arises from the fact that the hero or heroine's efforts do not always succeed. Spinoza called this phenomenon *conatus*, the pursuit of self-preservation. The effort (*conari* = to make an effort) one must make to maintain the self is a fundamental feature of being human. Consequently, it should not surprise anyone that storytelling (the plotting of events) very much involves the staging of efforts put into avoiding the contingencies of existence (Boullart 1999, 461–63).

The degradation narrative essentially mourns the suffering of humanity, the sad fact that someone's narrative about the course of his or her life always seems more or less inadequate or even illusionary. The suffering is due to people themselves because they are so vain as to believe that they can control the story pattern of a human life—think of Emma Bovary's tragic misunderstanding between real and imaginary desires or the suffering caused by the human condition. In all circumstances, humans are confronted with personal limitations: either the gods prove to be stronger, or the person turns out to be anything but a god possessing infallible knowledge and performing omnipotent actions.

From the perspective of the hero or heroine, the chronotope of degradation could be said to end in a conflict chronotope. Apart from this, it is easy to see that conflicts are crucial to tragedies. There is also the immense influence of coincidences and chance events. Laius, Oedipus's biological father, just happens to be on the same road his son is taking when the latter tries to escape the oracle's prophecy. Chance plays an even more distinct role in the works of Shakespeare.

> Shakespeare, lastly, in most of his tragedies allows "chance" or "accident" an appreciable influence at some point in the action. Chance or accident here will be found, I think, to mean any occurrence (not supernatural, of course) which enters the dramatic sequence neither from the agency of a character, nor from the obvious surrounding circumstances. (Bradley 1905, 14–15)[17]

The accidental character of Juliet's protracted apparent death, Desdemona's handkerchief appearing at far too coincidental moments, and the coincidence of Polonius's standing behind the curtain are all "accidental" events with the power to alter entire lives, and these events are abundant in Shakespeare's work. In other words, the negatively valued moral space not only permeates the catastrophe at the end of the story but also infiltrates right from the start in all sorts of conflicts.[18] In Shakespeare's *Othello*, one of the most important prototypes of the tragedy, everything initially goes the hero's way (a perfect military career, ideal love relationship, great social prestige). The malicious interventions of troublemakers, however, tear down this world, followed by conflicts occurring in rapid succession. This linear downfall is typical in the tragedy. It turns the genre into the prototype of all narratives in which failing heroes, heroines, and broken worlds bear witness to the depressing lack of equilibrium in the world of human experience.

CONVERSION IN THE REGENERATION CHRONOTOPE
The Hero's Moral Regeneration

What I have said about the nomothetic and the sacred ethos of the tragic hero or heroine on a mission only applies to a part of narrative culture. To assess the true value of the moral function of rascals in the classical travel novel (Apuleius, Petronius) and the picaresque narrative, or that of the powerless hero or heroine in horror stories and popular romances, we must introduce a second type of moral ethos. In these narratives, the hero or heroine hardly has any goal in mind while going through a chaotic series of experiences, thereby allowing us to designate the ethos as protean. In this sense, the regeneration chronotope manifests a more modern and more existential dimension. The modern dimension is found in an anti-dogmatic attitude; the existential dimension is an inclination toward a non–collectively defined, subjective way of finding meaning in the world. In short, the regeneration chronotope expresses an ethos in which the stream of life appears uncontrollable. The untouchable hero or heroine of the mission narrative, on the one hand, will use his or her sacred (superhuman and holy) ethos to *subdue* his or her surroundings (and the tragic hero will try to do this in vain). On the other hand, the more common, everyday hero or heroine of the regeneration chronotopes will *adapt* to these surroundings. As recipients, we do not enjoy the victory of the morally superior as much as we do the intelligence and persistence that go together with this adaptive ability. In other words, moral virtue inheres in the hero's or heroine's capacity to "come home" despite everything, in some narratives even without any moral effort. For example, in picaresque narratives, the emphasis is on the hero's or heroine's cunningness and the turnabout at the end is quasi-accidental. Other texts (such as those by Apuleius) suggest that the confrontation with vices leads to a point of saturation, or "tipping point," at which the turnabout becomes inevitable.

In this respect, Bakhtin argues that guilt, moral weakness, and fallacies are the forces that give the starting impetus to the travel narrative's action (1981a, 117). Since the seventeenth century, the turnabout in narratives employing regeneration chronotopes becomes a matter of repentance. Whereas in older texts the initiation into the "better life" happens almost spontaneously, the heroes and heroines of modern narratives are aware of their weaknesses and take more explicit action when repenting, reforming, or converting themselves. In this sense, it is repentance, reform, and conversion that provide the model of morality in the regeneration chronotope. William James, in one of his lectures on religion, describes the structure of this model as follows:

> To be converted, to be regenerated, to receive grace, to experience religion, to gain an assurance, are so many phrases which denote the process, gradual

or sudden, by which a self hitherto divided, and consciously wrong inferior and unhappy, becomes unified and consciously right superior and happy, in consequence of its firmer hold upon religious realities. This at least is what conversion signifies in general terms, whether or not we believe that a direct divine operation is needed to bring such a moral change about. (1902)

In the regeneration chronotope, the hero or heroine is the object of the initiation ritual: he or she faces the threat of a downfall owing to an inner and outer sinfulness but is eventually lifted to a higher level thanks to a mythical intervention. In short, the hero or heroine resembles the poet in the *Divina Commedia* who gradually undergoes an initiation in excellence. In the exact same way as in the mission chronotope, the hero or heroine is the plaything of the dialectical relationship between regularity and turmoil. The mission chronotope hero or heroine reiterates the mythical regularity and gives it its rightful place in the final moment (the pattern "regularity-turmoil-recurrent regularity"). In the case of the initiated hero or heroine, a sharp contrast exists between the turmoil of the sinful life and the regularity of the original state (the crisis-rebirth pattern).

Morality and Conflict for the Victim-Hero

The principal objective in regeneration chronotopes is either escaping or "manipulating" the threatening situation. Propp's ethnographical research reveals this type of ethos to be a prominent phenomenon, calling the characters who propagate this form of moral attitude the victim-heroes. A victim–hero/heroine is not a character who is charged with a task, but one who must give him- or herself a task because of his or her own situation—the goal being to escape the initial situation. This is the reason why the eschaton is often "negatively" defined, that is, as an evocation of the nonsinful, nonpetty human life. The conflict chronotopes adapt to this new eschaton. They become evocations of sinfulness and petty humanity. During their adventures, heroes and heroines go through a process of punishment that eventually culminates in a sort of salvation.[19]

The adventures of the victim–hero/heroine unfold in what Bakhtin calls the "adventure time of the second type" (1981a, 116). As opposed to the adventure time of the mission and degradation chronotope, the initiative here mainly lies with the hero or heroine and no longer solely with external fate.[20] Everyday life holds many interesting conflicts, for example, those in which life's "underbelly" shows itself. This is why obscene conflicts around sex, violence, and crime dominate the horror novel and romance, the picaresque novel and the classical travel narrative. Conflict situations of this sort are headed straight for the hero or heroine in a (perpetually extendable) series of episodes, so as to allow him or her to go through his or her development into a better person. During this development— seldomly represented in the form of psychological growth and especially mechanical in nature—the hero or heroine undergoes small metamorphoses. He or she is a protean hero or heroine, in the sense that he or she is continually adjusting his or her identity according to the conflict situations in which he or she appears. Protean, for that matter, is the concept (drawn from the metamorphoses of Proteus, the sea god) used to indicate a personality structure tuned to adjustment and change. With his or her protean nature, the hero or heroine of the regeneration chronotope is very different from the nomothetic attitude of the two preceding types of heroes and heroines: the character seems to possess several identities and will display these different identities in succession. Eventually, in the eschaton, the ultimate transformation takes place: the hero or heroine is reformed or converted and regenerates by laying aside all conflicts.

It is clear that the regeneration chronotope is not dominated by an absolute boundary that must be transgressed. There is no contrast between the alien and the familiar, which is the principal structural feature of the mission chronotope. Instead, alien and familiar spaces both prove to be recognizable and of an ordinary, common kind. There is no clear boundary but more of a sub-boundary. From the start, we find ourselves in the "external" space that the hero or heroine needs to delimit by creating a "home" or an "inside" within the "outside." The presence of small transformations and the absence of an absolute boundary demonstrate that the regeneration chronotope is the form of teleology that is the least oriented toward the mythical. The regeneration chronotope is far less tuned to the expectation of equilibrium, and is composed of scenes of disequilibrium. This is also demonstrated in later forms of the regeneration chronotope by the introduction of the gothic villain, who in the preromantic horror story receives the majority of attention as a hero or heroine embodying the negative (Richter 1994; Van Gorp 1998). The character of conflict even seems to be the narrative's protagonist rather than antagonist. This character is so dominant that the world seems to exist entirely through conflicts, and any possibility of evading them seems to have become impossible. In this sense, the gothic villain symbolizes the sub-boundary-situation.[21] A similar fixation on conflict and doom characterizes the genre of the popular romance. In stories of the well-liked Bride's Bouquet series, published by Mills and Boone, the majority of actions are a series of confrontations between the victim-heroine and an unrelenting and seemingly untrustworthy love interest.

Morality and Equilibrium in Comic Stories

In horror stories and romances, the emphasis is on the linear succession of coincidences and not on the confrontation with an absolute boundary. At the end of each scene, some sort of pause is usually inserted, a moment at which the danger or the negative emotion seems averted (see the above-mentioned small transformations). A definitive state of equilibrium, however, is by no means achieved; for the duration of the story, the state of turmoil is latently present. The only traces of a mythical dimension's presence are given by, for example, the hopeful signs the heroine recognizes in her future lover. Occasionally, the story shows a glimpse of regularity, as though to give the impression that something is definitely emerging; that "emergence" is the answer to all states of turmoil and danger (which, in a play on words, could be called *emergency* situations). In the regeneration chronotope, equilibrium and regularity are mostly accidental. The emphasis in the regeneration chronotope is on the linear chain of coincidences, and when a state of equilibrium is involved, it is little more than a type of award or reward for the turmoil suffered. Essentially, these narratives do not revolve around the longing for the great equilibrium of the entire world; instead, they revolve around the small equilibriums that are within the reach of the individual. Nevertheless, it is the great equilibrium that eventually will close off the narrative. In all cases, the narrative indeed celebrates the hero's or heroine's homecoming, a clear demonstration of the fact that the pains suffered were mere stages of an initiation within a mysterious eschatological plan. I can illustrate this with a quotation from King's *The Shining*:

> The woman was sitting on the porch in a rocking chair, a book in her hands. Hallorann was struck again by the change in her. Part of it was the stiff, almost formal way she sat, in spite of her informal surroundings—that was the back brace, of course. She'd had a shattered vertebra as well as three broken ribs and some internal injuries. The back was the slowest healing, and she was still in the brace . . . hence the formal posture. But the change was more than that. She looked older, and some of the laughter had gone out of her face. Now, as she sat reading her book, Hallorann saw a grave sort of beauty there that had been missing on the day he had first met her, some nine months ago. Then she had still been mostly girl. Now she was a woman, a human being who had been dragged around to the dark side of the moon and had come back able to put the pieces back together. But those pieces, Hallorann thought, they never fit just the same way again. Never in this world. (1977, 442–43)

Variations on this type of closing scene can be found in the profundities uttered in the final parts of some of the earliest novels (for example, by Apuleius) and the picaresque novel. When the hero or heroine suddenly enters the harmonious world (monastery, citizen life) at the end of the narrative, it appears that the world is (finally) exhibiting a certain moral order.

In popular variants of the regeneration plot, the desire for regularity and equilibrium noticeably play a more significant part. Narratives belonging to the genre of the popular romance or horror novel tend to stage such extreme forms of turmoil (love sickness, fear) that the story arc is automatically steered in the direction of a future equilibrium. It is true that any reference to a preceding equilibrium is absent, and only few descriptions of instances of equilibrium are given throughout the narrative, yet not a moment passes in which the tension is not clearly building up to a future state of equilibrium.

A Typology of Dialogical Chronotopes

TRAGICOMIC TENDENCIES IN MODERN NARRATIVE CULTURE

In a certain sense, almost *all* traditional stories are tragicomic. Because all stories contain elegiac and idyllic elements, they are by definition bittersweet. In *The Mind and Its Stories*, Hogan distinguishes three prototypical plot structures, arguing that the tragic and the comic mode occur simultaneously in the majority of cases. His impressive body of epic stories proves that representations of harmony (the comic end of a story arc) constantly appear in conjunction with representations of turmoil and contingency (the tragic aspect of a story arc).[22] The epithet bittersweet, however, is claimed with greater legitimacy by modern dialogical narrative art. In the course of the modern narrative, a permanent sense of ambivalence is conveyed because the stories do not pass a priori judgments about the world and its intentionality, and because the object of this intentionality has vanished from the narrative's end. This ambivalence is tied up with two phenomena. On the one hand, the tragic and comic effects are caused by psychological forces that continually intersect in a character's world. On the other hand, these effects can be explained by the juxtaposition of the tragic and comic trajectories of different characters in the totality of the narrative world.

Dialogical chronotopes consist of junctions of psychological forces and are the result of the "empathetic examination of individual consciences" (Pavel 2006, 4). The interiorized tension between conflict and equilibrium causes the junction to drift alternately toward situations of conflict that evoke an elegiac mood and an idyllic state of equilibrium.[23] Narratives employing teleological chronotopes arrest this uninterrupted interaction between equilibrium and conflict by giving it a clear orientation and, more importantly, a goal. Because of this, and viewed from the perspective of the plot-space chronotope, these teleological chronotopes' characters are invariable.

> In the majority of subcategories of the novel, the plot, composition and entire internal structure of the novel postulate this unchanging nature, this solidity of the hero's image, this static nature of his unity. The hero is a constant in the novel's formula and all other quantities—the spatial environment, social position, fortune, in brief, all aspects of the hero's life and destiny—can therefore be variables. (Bakhtin 1986, 21)

In dialogical narratives, the relationship is the other way round: the hero or heroine turns out to be a variable and his or her environment shows a series of invariable traits. This reversal is most visible in the nineteenth century, when novelists
came to realize that individuals tend to be shaped by their social and historical
environment more than by moral norms (Pavel 2006, 3). That being said, there is
a long tradition of writers examining the ways in which the human psyche reacts
to its environment and the amount of freedom that humanity could claim. Indeed,
the cardinal question of modern Western narrative culture is "whether humans
are the source of moral law and masters of their own actions" (Pavel 2006, 3).
The answer soon proved to be relative: sometimes regeneration seems possible,
sometimes humans are degraded to a will-less plaything of an otherwise indifferent
universe. Conflict and equilibrium are anchored in the characters and the tension
between both, which leads to the conclusion that the return to harmony as well
as the departure from harmony are inherent to the human psyche. At the end of
The Portrait of a Lady, Isabel returns to Osmond, the man who brought her happiness and doom. At the end of *Crime and Punishment*, Raskolnikov's doubt diminishes
(he reports himself to the police), and he faces a bleak existence in Siberia. At the
same time, however, Sonia follows him, and his fate is thought to be a matter of
reconciliation. The reason for the tragicomic endings is evident: these narratives
deal with the human condition, the psychological fate of man, precluding the possibility of apodictic statements about the world.

The Raskolnikov-Sonia duo demonstrates that dialogical narratives typically
possess a twofold feature: regeneration and degradation not only become interiorized tendencies but also play against each other in the composition of the plot-
space. Characters who succeed in coming to grips with their moral, emotional,
and cognitive life are often contrasted with characters who do not succeed in this.
The technique of contrasting, in close keeping with the tendency to psychologize,
borrows dialogical narratives from drama. On the one hand, modern tragic poets,
such as Shakespeare, exert a heavy influence on modern writers of prose. On the
other hand, there is great respect for the way in which bourgeois popular culture
deals with personal, moral problems—this is especially true for melodrama, in-
vented around 1800 in postrevolutionary France and extremely popular in the
nineteenth century. Writers such as Balzac ventured to do projects commissioned
by boulevard theaters. It is, however, more important to consider the way in which
Balzac's "serious" work is guided by melodramatic techniques.

> Melodrama represents both the urge toward resacralization and the im-
> possibility of conceiving sacralization other than in personal terms. Melo-
> dramatic good and evil are highly personalized; they are assigned to, they
> inhabit persons who indeed have no psychological complexity but who are
> strongly characterized. . . . The ritual of melodrama involves the confron-

tation of clearly identified antagonists and the expulsion of one of them. (Brooks 1995, 16, 17)

The resemblance between melodrama and dialogically conceived novels can be explained by the conflict's predilection for psychological material. By staging relationships of tension between psychological junctions, modern narrative art is able to continue imparting a moral message in postsacred times. Although modern men and women are unable to deduce values from a "transcendental system of belief" (Brooks 1995: viii), they are still fascinated by the great conflict between good and evil. Melodrama differs because of the way in which moral conflicts are elaborated. The fact is that when a dialogical narrative juxtaposes a character of degradation and a character of regeneration, this does not yet imply that the narrative is combining two teleological chronotopes. After all, the successful regeneration or the failure of a character remains a psychological issue, which does not entirely fill the plot-space. The final point and the ultimate goal of the narrative in many instances remain "empty" spaces.[24] Together with the fundamentally tragicomic nature of dialogical narratives and the desacralization of morality, goal-orientedness and eschatology are pushed into the background. Certainly, the characters are uninterruptedly involved in problem-solving and intentional, goal-directed actions, perhaps even more so in Western narrative culture. Their projects, however, only very rarely arrive at a conclusion. Modern literary men and women simply detest rounded off lives. Peter Rabinowitz states that

> one of the primary targets for many nineteenth- and twentieth-century novelists has been closure itself. . . . I would argue that many realistic writers prefer endings in which the full consequences of the events portrayed . . . are neither worked out nor clearly implied. (2002, 307)

He detects the process not only in *Crime and Punishment*, in *Pelléas and Mélisande*, but also—and this is in keeping with Brooks's analyses in *The Melodramatic Imagination*—in the novels of Balzac and James, which truly excel in unresolved endings. These novels stage personalities and psyches, and most of the dramatic action is created by the psychological tension *between* and *within* the characters.

Nonetheless, the fact remains that every reader is under the impression that the modern novel leads to a certain goal. Indeed, it is often possible to observe causal connections in a series of events unfolding around one single character. Madame Bovary's path of life, which dominates Flaubert's novel, can without a single doubt be called tragic.

Apparently, it is possible to pass unambiguous judgments about the nature of the dialogical chronotope. The reason for this is that the tragicomic endings of dialogical narratives are accompanied by insights about the human condition of the characters. Both readers and characters are alerted to the moral, emotional, and intellectual conditions of their existence. The insight gained is incomplete and far from overpowering but nonetheless offers something to consider. As was the case with teleological narrative, the integral image of the plot-space is translated into judgments about the fictional world and the events that take place in it. Whereas teleological narratives enabled the subdivision of genres based on the plot-space's structure, categorizations of genres for dialogical stories can only be based on the judgments that are present *in*, and are passed by the recipient *about*, the junctions of the dialogical plot-space. Specifically, the moments of disclosure constitute a possible foundation for arriving at subdivisions of genres. An initial impetus to such a theory of genres is offered by Moretti, who demonstrates that some works give cause for a harmonious representation of moral norms (by way of the ideals of normalcy behind the characters) and that others propagate a skeptical or even cynical view of norms. The former category, narratives with a Hegelian classification plot, can be called comic. The latter category, owing to its Darwinian transformation plot, tends toward the elegiac, tragic mode. Only those narratives in which the reader is unable to form an opinion about the moral judgment are ambiguous because there is not a single junction present (character) that could induce such a judgment. These narratives are called tragicomic.[25]

TWO FORMS OF AGNITION

In order to distinguish the comic variants of the dialogical chronotope from the tragic variants, we can introduce a genre criterion that is frequently applied in the interpretation of dialogical narratives. By examining the ways in which the different protagonists arrive at agnition, it is possible to track down the differences between narratives. Agnition is Moretti's translation of the Aristotelian concept of *disclosure* (*anagnorisis*[26])—the revelation of truth and values in a narrative (Moretti 1983, 159–62). Disclosure is crucial in modern stories because these pay a great deal of attention to processes of consciousness-awakening and consciousness-raising in the design of their particular networks; therefore, modern stories have apparently learned much from the designers of degradation chronotopes. Consider the modern writer who looks at classical tragedy for instructions on how to raise tension through the staging of a psychological evolution. In the dialogical chronotope, however, disclosure is not as easily determined in an unambiguous way as in, for example, the classical tragedy. The reason for this resides in the tragicomic tendency of these narratives. First, there is the fact that in many narratives different characters simultaneously arrive at disclosures—in other words, that most narratives have a "complex plot" (O'Neill 2005, 368). This causes the narrative to look like a space of intersecting plot lines, making it necessary to represent it in the form of a network. Second, in all modern narratives disclosure assumes the form of a gradual process. The disclosure itself is a network of instances of disclosure, the larger part of which needs to be interconnected for us to be able to come to grips with the narrative. Because of the tragicomic nature of the dialogical chronotope, disclosure unfolds at multiple moments. Frye has indicated this by stating that more complex stories are virtually indifferent to the narrative's ending and frequently leave aside the question "how is this story going to turn out?" (1973, 52). The events are not instantly related to the integral plot development but are connected to a moral question: "what's the point of this story?" (Frye 1973, 52). The recipient experiences the world from the point of view of the character, and this leads to insecurity with respect to the objective and the moral value or the causes of the events. In a classical tragedy, the disclosure of an eschaton progresses in a linear and unambiguous manner. The disclosure through moments of kairos, however, is situated at the junctions, while the narrative is keeping up an uninterrupted psychological tension. It is no accident that kairos is represented as a god carrying wings at the heels and on the back (the deciding moment is gone in the blink of the eye), and a tuft on his head (as the German expression goes: *die gelegenheit beim schopf packen*, "to seize the opportunity"—literally: "to seize the opportunity by the tuft"). The kairos is the moment in which disclosure is *possible* but definitely not necessary. In the larger part of the dialogical narrative, opportunities fail to be seized, and chances are lost.

This method of working presents a sharp contrast with the traditional narratives. The truth revealed by Sherlock Holmes is based on an a priori value forming the *raison d'être* of the narrative: crime must be punished. In other words, the revelation of the morally despicable act is little more than the confirmation of something that was unveiled. Dialogical stories operate with gradual revelation. Whenever a glimpse of the answer appears in a moment of crisis, we draw nearer to the disclosure of the narrative's moral pattern. We repeatedly go through an "aha-experience" and have our minds increasingly focused on the network's junctions. In this sense, the narrative is like a revue of multiple emotions, behavioral guidelines, and ideas from which, at the end of the process of disclosure, the most desirable affect, the ideal attitude, or the correct view emerges. The difference between elementary and complex forms of disclosure is aptly expressed in a remark on the picaresque novel by René Wellek and Austin Warren:

> In the picaresque novel, the chronological sequence is all there is: this happened and then that. . . . A more philosophical novel adds to chronology the structure of causation. (1976, 222)

In conceiving and receiving narratives, the focus of attention will spontaneously turn to the moment at which the disclosure process is complete, the moment at which the causal structure of the psychological development allows an overall judgment. Moretti calls this moment, which constitutes the *point* of a dialogically composed narrative, the moment of agnition.[27] The narrative is said to have reached its zenith when change has become impossible, the moment at which the disclosure process has arrived at the point of no return. The moment of agnition in dialogical chronotopes typically results from the psychological process of disclosure that I have described above. However, this final point does not really close the debate because the relationship with other affects, attitudes, and views must be respected until the end. If the scene of Madame Bovary's death must be interpreted, then her previous positions must also be taken into account because they are, after all, the elements of a network of which the scene of her death is merely the "last disclosure." This is also true for fairly simple forms of dialogical chronotopes. At the end of *Imitation of Life*, Douglas Sirk's classic melodrama, a disobedient daughter repents, and (in a second plot) a character aspiring to be an actress finally gains insight into her frenetic desire for success. Both choose in favor of family values and shake off their confused emotional state. The disclosure does not fall from the sky but is carefully prepared through a network of moments of kairos. The "disobedient" daughter needs a number of those situations to gain insight. At the same time, the "intemperate" aspiring actress lives her moments of crisis. The example demonstrates that a dialogical chronotope's network is a very multi-faceted and fairly ambiguous construct. As demonstrated in Sirk's melodrama, the dialogical chronotope consists of multiple processes of disclosure and multiple moments of agnition.

When we are confronted with a dominant character and a dominant process of disclosure in a narrative, this leads to a feeling of satisfaction and to a comic effect. When this is not the case, the narrative leaves a tragic impression. When there is both a dominant character who undergoes an evolution in the tragic sense and another character who undergoes an evolution in the comic sense, then this narrative can be called tragicomic. In these cases, the characters' moments of agnition do not lead to an unambiguous moment of agnition for the recipient, thus rendering it impossible to subsume the narrative under a particular genre category. It is striking, then, to observe that a different moral attitude comes to the fore in the tragic and comic forms of the dialogical chronotope. Because moral values in dialogical narratives are essentially obscured, the *nature* of the process of disclosure is of great significance.[28] If in the course of the process of inquiry and disclosure the answers to the moral problem remain forthcoming, then the narrative conveys a different message than when it divulges moral values (or the truth about a certain form of moral behavior).

In his later work, Moretti lucidly elaborated this relationship between agnition and morality. In his study about the bildungsroman, which will serve as a guideline, he demonstrated that modern literature does not posit any a priori norms or values. Instead, it raises the issue of morality by asking questions about characters who either achieve some degree of normality or do not. The difference between the classification plot and the transformation plot refers to that polarity of normalcy. If a character becomes aware that his or her behavior can be submitted to norms ("normalized"), then the narrative appeals more than anything to the comic variant of the dialogical chronotope. If this is not the case, if normality is questioned, then the process of transformation of the hero or heroine (the process of disclosure) leads to the denial of normality and to a tragic plot-space.

COMIC AND TRAGIC FORMS OF AGNITION
In his analysis of the classification plot, Moretti concentrates on the taxonomy of social phenomena that dominates this sort of narrative. Initially, the classification seems to fall short, but the characters transform in such a way that they succeed in achieving a different, this time definitive, classification. The narrative is stabilized through the process of disclosure and, eventually, by way of the moment of agnition. In other words, the comic evolution of the plot can be retraced to the fact that a dominant character (usually the leading character chosen by the recipient) achieves a certain form of equilibrium.

States of psychological equilibrium (moments of happiness, interiorized idylls) are the ones most frequently discussed in modern stories.[29] The quest for happiness in comic stories tends to preserve the status quo in society. An aversion to chance and change predominate, even if the desire for security and happiness is at the expense of freedom. In these narratives, the heroes and heroines gradually arrive at a psychological equilibrium because they succeed in discovering a stable classification, an efficient moral order in their surroundings. According to Moretti, this kind of hero or heroine performs a Hegelian maneuver of thought. During the moment of agnition, he or she concludes that the difficulties encountered during the course of the narrative—a conflict with another character, mutual frustration, isolation—were but a detour to render possible the ideal classification of his or her world.[30] On the mental level (in the world of thinking, wanting, and feeling), something happens to the characters, which then generates a situation we could call an equilibrium chronotope: a source of misunderstanding is eliminated; the character is ready to compromise or acknowledge feelings that he or she formerly avoided. In the end, the process of disclosure, by way of a marriage or some other form of social harmony, results in the character's decision to embrace the normative culture and lead a life of "normality."

Moretti's analysis corresponds with the view held by other plot theorists. Many novels, classified by Crane under the headings of "plots of character" and "plots of thought," can be subsumed under the category of "classification plot." The same applies to Friedman's summation of the subcategories of both types: "the maturing plot" (Charles Dickens's *Great Expectations*), "the reform plot" (Nathaniel Hawthorne's *The Scarlet Letter*), "the testing plot" (Samuel Richardson's *Pamela*). The aforementioned novels serve as examples for a plot of character in which moral values change, whereas "the education plot" (Mark Twain's *The Adventures of Huckleberry Finn*), "the revelation plot" (Roald Dahl's "Beware of the Dog"), and "the affective plot" (Jane Austen's *Pride and Prejudice*) serve as examples of a plot with transformations of ideas.

Additionally, there is a great similarity between Moretti's classification plot and the four types of the bildungsroman mentioned by Bakhtin in his study on the subject. He refers to the novels of Theodor Gottlieb von Hippel, Jean Paul, and Tolstoy to show that many bildungsromans present heroes and heroines who gradually achieve a state of harmony in their lives. In this process, individual happiness seems to go together with some form of social harmony. A second series of novels examined by Bakhtin describes the process of growing up and reaching maturity. In these narratives (Gottfried Keller's *Der grüne Heinrich* [*Green Heinrich*], Dickens's *Oliver Twist*), the hero goes through adolescence in difficult circumstances and changes his ambitions depending on the situations of conflict he encounters along the way (Bakhtin 1986, 23). A third series of novels that can be understood through the concept of the Hegelian classification plot consists of narratives in which the moral transformation of a hero or heroine is shown in a pseudo-biographical fashion (Henry Fielding's *Tom Jones* and Dickens's *David Copperfield*). A fourth series of examples comprises the educational bildungsromans (*Erziehungsromans*), such as, for example, Rousseau's *Emile*.[31] What is at stake in these narratives is always the same: the individual must be able to hold his own in a web of relationships and in spite of chaotic and conflicting impressions. As Bakhtin puts it in his study of chronotopes:

> A man must educate or re-educate himself for life in a world that is, from his point of view, enormous and foreign; he must make it his own, domesticate it. In Hegel's definition, the novel must educate man for life in bourgeois society. (1981a, 234)

Central to modern narrative culture is the tension between the characters who see themselves as junctions of psychological forces and who entertain a problematic relationship with external forces in society. Consequently, the problem is often a battle between the ideal of individual freedom and societal normalcy. Will the character decide to be integrated into society or will he or she allow him- or herself to be forced into isolation? In the Hegelian classification plot, the character chooses in favor of harmony and equilibrium and leaves behind all potential conflicts: "the clash between individual autonomy and social integration" becomes the cause for the "elusion of whatever may endanger the Ego's equilibrium" (Moretti 1987, 12). The character voluntarily submits to the moral law of his or her community and will, in fact, shy away from individual freedom.

The image of the escape from freedom, which places the desire to "belong" within the individual psyche itself, is, as it were, its solution. . . . Socialization is no longer felt as a mere necessity but as a value choice: it has become "legitimate." (Moretti 1987, 67)

A completely different option is found in the Darwinian transformation plot. The novels Moretti had in mind when coining the concept are the great bildungsromans published after 1800; not surprisingly, these are the very same novels to which Bakhtin pays the greatest attention. The fact is that Bakhtin attempts to show that the perfect dialogicity can only be realized in a narrative culture in which the nuclear position is occupied not by answers but by questions. In the Goethean bildungsroman, and in the nineteenth-century tradition elaborating on it, Bakhtin (and Moretti) detect a critical form of narrative culture. Here, characters enter into a dialogue with a reality that has become problematic because it has become historical, changeable, and, consequently, relative. As Lukács expresses it in *Theory of the Novel*, center stage in the modern novel is taken by the problematic hero or heroine. The protagonist in the bourgeois novel seeks meaning and values, and during this quest, he or she is confronted with a "godforsaken world" (as Hegel expressed it in his *Introductory Lectures on Aesthetics*) lacking any absolute system of values. According to literary sociologists such as Lukács, a clear connection can be observed between the novel and modernity. Western narrative art is thematically integrated by its confrontation with social phenomena such as the fragmentation of social relationships and systems of symbolic meaning. Characters perceive this historical tendency of moving away from tradition to be problematic. Owing to the absence of faith in an absolute creational plan, every single action becomes relative, involving characters frenetically seeking values in a seemingly norm-ridden world.[32] Hence, they no longer spread the idea of normality, which continues to dominate comic stories.[33]

This is where Moretti situates the decisive contrast with the comic type. In the novels of Stendhal, Pushkin, Balzac, and Flaubert, the characters are dominated by an uncontrollable web of relationships. The hero or heroine, having to hold his or her own in a world of coincidences and masquerades, does not exhibit the slightest indication of unambiguous behavior. The culmination of this tendency is to be found in the "novel of adultery," which recounts "an existence devoted to instability" (Moretti 1987). Sure enough, the heroes and heroines are dynamic, oozing a restless energy. Yet these dynamics do not in the least result in maturity. For a hero such as Fréderique Moreau, maturity is identical to betrayal, and (the illusion of) safety is completely wasted on him. In the course of the narrative, heroes and heroines may go through an evolution because they participate in several historical transformations; however, their adventures lead to anything but agnition.

The tragic variant of the dialogical chronotope remains the one most cherished by literary theorists. Western culture's transformation narratives are indeed hymns to the refusal to be integrated into society. This refusal is not merely a matter of acts and omissions. It also represents an intellectual attitude. Modern heroes and heroines of the tragic type are as wary of collaborating with the powers that be as they are of any coercion into normalcy. In a sense, they oppose every external organization of their plan of life and offer resistance to the teleological tendencies of the psyche. Much like Hamlet, they choose to cultivate their *kairophobia*.

Notes

Introduction

1. Memory's preference for pictures or words highly charged with imagery can be partly explained by the fact that the images they evoke contain complex information that is available simultaneously; thus, two units of information in one image take up the same amount of space in memory as one word without an image (Paivio 1983, 9).

2. "Elle présente des situations futures, ou de pure fantaisie, elle découvre, elle invente" (English translation by Jo Smets).

3. "Le pouvoir d'inventer qui est en nous ne porte pas seulement sur des combinaisons d'images, mais sur des idées, des jugements. Par 'imagination' il faut donc entendre toute pensée en excercise, contemplant ou combinant des matériaux représentatifs. L'imagination, c'est la pensée même" (English translation by Jo Smets).

4. Darko Suvin—by no coincidence an expert on adventure stories (science fiction)—anticipated very early the pragmatic turn in narratology by connecting the theory of possible worlds with Bakhtin's thought. "The PW [possible world] is constructed by the reader's ideologically restrained imagination, it is a signified and representamen, to be clearly distinguished from the text surface, which is a signifier and representans" (Suvin 1989, 40).

5. Literary, film, and performing arts theorists routinely study the effects of stories but reduce these to the themes or ideas derived from the story by the recipient. These abstracta, Bakhtin says (1981a, 250), cannot be studied without taking into account the imaginal strategies that precede them. In his study of the transcendental conditions of the perception of film images, Deleuze put this principle into practice by connecting C. S. Peirce's pragmatic semiotics (specifically his theory about the sign functions ascribed to the interpretant mechanisms) with philosophical reflections about "time." It is this road I would like to follow, even if the semiotic aspect is only given space *en sourdine* and Bakhtin's theory of chronotopes is the object of attention. In this study, the question "what does it mean?" makes room for a new question: "how does it work?" (Deleuze 1972, 130). Entering a dialogue with one of Deleuze's most important works, *L'Anti-Oedipe* (1972), Roland Barthes aptly expressed the effect of art: "The pleasure of the text is that moment when my body pursues its own ideas—for my body does not have the same ideas I do" (1975, 16–17). Barthes refers to an experiential process that

every lover of art experiences as evident yet that has hardly been discussed by art theories.

6. These neologisms are somewhat tautological. In an *action-space,* "action" represents "time"; in a *plot-space,* "plot" represents time development; and in a *worldview,* time and space are evidently implied. Adding "chronotope" in this sense is somewhat redundant. Nevertheless, it is important to emphasize that these terms concern effects of imagination. Because the term chronotope perfectly expresses this, it is added to the concepts of action-space, plot-space, and worldview.

Chapter 1

1. Mitterand—along with Morson—argues that "the theory of chronotopes is more a theory of novelistic time than it is one of novelistic space. . . . It is time that dynamizes and dialecticizes space; and in the story/narrative, it is time that dynamizes description as well as narration" (Mitterand 1990, 182; English translation by Jo Smets). [la théorie du chronotope est une théorie du temps romanesque plus que de l'espace romanesque. (. . .) C'est le temps qui dynamise et dialectise l'espace; et dans le récit, c'est le temps qui dynamise la description aussi bien que la narration.]

2. This view of narratives as representations of human activities is in keeping with the questions asked by Bakhtin in his study of chronotopes. Pam Morris identifies "the aesthetic visualizing of a human being in relation to their temporal and spatial world" as the central concern of this essay (1994, 180). Morson and Emerson also mention a few problems that are fairly Aristotelian in nature: "What is the relation of human action to its context? Is the context mere background, or does it actively shape events? Are actions dependent to a significant degree on where or when they occur?" (1990, 169).

3. Deleuze comes to the same conclusion in his work on cinematic imagination. In the chapter on the action-image, he states: "what constitutes realism is simply this: milieux and modes of behaviour, milieux which actualise and modes of behaviour which embody. The action-image is the relation between the two and all the varieties of this relation" (1986, 145).

4. For narratologists, "plot" represents one of three ways of defining a narrative. Manfred Jahn states: "Ideally, one should distinguish *three* action-related aspects: (i) the sequence of events as ordered in the discourse; (ii) the action as it happened in its actual chronological sequence (= story); and (iii) the story's causal structure (= plot)" (2005, 42). According to Ricoeur, the causal structure controlling the events in a narrative is the most important realization of "time" in a narrative, which is also the reason why I prefer this term.

5. Gabriel Zoran was one of the first to argue that every narrative space is

permeated by time: "[I use the term *chronotopos*] not to signify all things that may be found in space or in time, but only what may be defined by an integration of spatial and temporal categories as movement and change. One may thus speak of the effect of the *chronotopos* on the structure of space" (1984, 318).

6. On this level, too, Zoran proved to be a pioneer. Apart from discussing chronotopic aspects of the narrative space (here called "action-space"), he also talks about the topographical space (Zoran 1984). For an example of this being applied to literary images of the city, see Keunen 2000.

7. For a narratological description of space in narrative texts, see Herman 2002, 263–99.

8. A more recent formulation of the narrative space as a space of relationships can be found in Marie-Laure Ryan (2003). She considers the imaginal representation of a narrative space to be a cognitive map and defines it as "a mental model of spatial relations."

9. For Bakhtin, the chronotope of the chivalric romance is so wondrous and alien that the reader does not expect anything other than the "unexpected" (1981a, 152). The chronotope of the Greek romance is designated in the same way as an "abstract-alien world" (1981a, 101). Here, "abstract" does not refer to the nature of the space as much as it does to the narrators' inclination to gear their world to concrete events that are recognized by the reader. Narratologically speaking, however, this type of spatial image can also be called "abstract."

10. Classical narratology argues as follows: "by clustering events in different spaces oppositions may arise" (Van Luxemburg 1981, 190). Oppositions are analyzed on the narrative level (subject, discourse) by relating them to semantic oppositions on the level of history (fabula, story), for example, an opposition between "inside" and "outside" (Bal 1978, 49–50). Weisgerber argues that coded spatial relations (spatial polarities) form indications of fundamental thematic elements, but at the same time, he warns against overrating their significance because it is incorrect that "every structure is decomposed in a series of oppositions" (1978, 228; English translation by Jo Smets). [toute structure se décompose en une série d'oppositions.]

11. When Bakhtin, at the end of his study of chronotopes, states that the chronotopes of the road, the salon, or the gothic castle function "as the primary means for materializing time in space" (1981a, 250), he is referring to the interaction between two levels. Here, time is the historical time at the level of the worldview, whereas the materialization occurs on the level of the action-space.

12. In fact, Bakhtin is concerned with a kind of hermeneutics of the imagination. According to Bruner, any theory of narrativity must inevitably result in such an endeavor. It is impossible to consume stories without the hermeneutic circle: "The object of hermeneutic analysis is to provide a convincing and non-contradictory account of what a story means, a reading in keeping with the

particulars that constitute it. This creates the famous 'hermeneutic circle'—trying to justify the 'rightness' of one reading of a text not by reference to the observable world or the laws of necessary reason, but by reference to other alternative readings. . . . Since the meanings of the parts of a story are 'functions' of the story as a whole, and, at the same time, the story as a whole depends for its formation upon appropriate constituent parts, story interpretation seems irretrievably hermeneutic. A story's parts and its whole must, as it were, be made to live together. And when a story captures our interest, we cannot resist the temptation to make its parts do so. That is what creates narrative's hermeneutic compulsion" (Bruner 1986, 138).

13. Actions occurring in narratives could be said to function as mnemonic cues. In recollecting stories, Paivio writes, it is essential that "the imaginal information is properly organized to begin with and that one has ready access to the image through a mnemonic cue" (1983, 10). The structure of the imaginal entities populating fictional stories is organized in such a manner that upon remembering the narrative, we automatically recall the characters' actions. This is also shown by more recent research dealing with identification: Oatley 1994, Neill 1996, Gaut 1999.

14. "From the situation of a subject whose existence is defined by deeds, time and space have the most immediate significance, in so far as they always give a final contour to his or her project" (Holquist 1990, 154). Bakhtin's perception of this arose from an encounter he had with neuropsychologist Oechtomsky in 1925. Given his fascination around this time with the role played by evaluations in the perception of the world, this action-theoretical perspective was of tremendous importance in the development of his thoughts. "[T]ime or space can never occur (or 'be') alone, but always constitute an event in which time (or space) exists only when coupled with a value" (Holquist 1990, 154).

15. Similar narratological entities are found in Jahn's "minimal sequence of events" (Jahn 2005, N4.2); a motif (in the terminology of Russian Formalists like Tomasjevski and Veselovski); and Dorfman's "action unit" or narreme, which appears in clusters that can be called "episodes" (Jahn 2005, N4.4). On the level of psychology, these units go hand in hand with an "episode schema" (Van Dijk and Kintsch 1983, 57). This concept, also used by Schank, goes back to Thorndyke's classical definition: "an episode schema might consist of a protagonist, a goal, an attempt by the protagonist to achieve the goal, and an outcome of the attempt" (Thorndyke and Yekovich 1980, 27).

16. Conversely, cognitivists believe texts can be considered as "sets of instructions to construe mental models" (Meutsch 1986, 319). These mental models can occur in different gradations. Schank, for example, works with the concept of "MOP" (memory organization package); Kintsch and Van Dijk work with "situation models," which are combinations of simpler schemas (Van Dijk and Kintsch 1983, 310).

17. Compare with "A chronotopic motif is . . . a sort of 'congealed event,'

and a chronotopic place is a sort of condensed reminder of the kind of time and space that typically functions there" (Morson and Emerson 1990, 374).

18. This view of narrative imagination expresses what every reader or film spectator intuitively experiences while consuming stories. It is hard to demonstrate the manner in which the levels of imagination interlock or interconnect. In the 1970s and 1980s, however, empirical narrative scientists (Thorndyke, for example) carried out some experiments confirming the episodic nature of narrative imagination. Van Dijk and Kintch offer an overview of these results, concluding that "episodes function as psychological units in story comprehension as well as recall" (1983, 57).

19. Bakhtin is certainly aware of this distinction. A key passage is the introduction to the part of his study of chronotopes that was added later. In it he explicitly states that the "scope" and "degree" of a chronotope can be mutually very different. Previous to his discussion of imaginal constructs on the level of the action-space (the chronotope of the gothic castle, of the salon, etc.), he argues: "Art and literature are shot through with chronotopic values of varying degree and scope. Each motif, each separate aspect of artistic work bears value. In these chapters we have analyzed only the major chronotopes that endure as types and that determine the most important generic variations on the novel in the early stages of its development. As we draw our essay to a close we will simply list, and merely touch upon, certain other chronotopic values having different degree and scope" (1981a, 243).

20. Brooks repeatedly returns to this in his study. "The sense of a beginning, then, must in some important way be determined by the sense of an ending. We might say that we are able to read present moments—in literature and, by extension, in life—as endowed with narrative meaning only because we read them in anticipation of the structuring power of those endings that will retrospectively give them the order and significance of plot" (Brooks 1984, 94). From his fairly narrow description of what makes reading so attractive, it is clear that Brooks overemphasizes what I call "teleological chronotopics." "The desire of the text (the desire of reading) is hence desire for the end, but desire for the end reached only through the at least minimally complicated detour, the intentional deviance, in tension, which is the plot of narrative" (Brooks 1984, 104).

21. Holquist rightly notes that in Bakhtin's work worldviews are not any vaguer than what literary sociology calls "ideologies." Bakhtin only uses those elements of worldviews (time and space) that enable us to explain ideologies. "But what is often overlooked is that there is not only a 'political unconscious,' but what might be called a 'chronotopic unconscious,' a set of unspoken assumptions about the coordinates of our experience so fundamental that they lie even deeper (and therefore may ultimately be more determining) than the prejudices imposed by ideology. In fact the two may be coterminous" (Holquist 1990, 141–42).

22. This theory of genre was highly successful in gender studies, spawning analyses of "the mother-daughter plot" or "the tested woman plot."

23. These two plot types correspond to the mission and regeneration chronotopes, a distinction I will propose in the third chapter.

Chapter 2

1. Bakhtin stresses that the preference for a certain concept of time in a story persists on several levels of the imagination. This thought has only rarely been considered in commentaries. Morson and Emerson are an exception, when they stress that "different aspects or orders of the universe cannot be supposed to operate with the same chronotope" (1990, 368).

2. Pearce correctly calls this phenomenon "polychronotopy," by analogy with Bakhtin's concept of "polyphony" (Pearce 1994, 174 ff.).

3. "This brings us to the question of the place of Aion in Greek philosophy. Here the essential significance is life-force, the vital spirit. On the one hand he is identified with the heavens or the cosmos, on the other he is creator of the absolute, eternal and divine nature. It is with this concept in mind that we must read the inscription on a statue of Aion found at Eleusis and dedicated in the time of Augustus: 'to the might of Rome and the perpetuation of the mysteries.' This Aion is a divine character who 'by his holy nature remains ever the same, who has no beginning or end, undergoes no change and who is the begetter of the divine nature'" (Farvardyn Project 2010).

4. In a sense, "unrest" compensates for the undesirable side effects of our longing for balance. Restless excitement or agitation pierces the boredom arising from the repetitiveness of a balanced situation (Cawelti 1976, 16). In our craving for fictional fear and insecurity, for the excitement of the fictional risk, of the new and the mysterious, we express that we simply need variation and alternation in order to exist. Umberto Eco rightfully says that every human being once in a while longs to feel like Superman, certainly when the greater part of life amounts to nothing but boredom (1988, 221). In this respect, we closely resemble rats in behavioral psychology experiments, readily allowing ourselves to be stimulated to the point of exhaustion.

5. "Repetition has as its function to make the structure of myth apparent" (Lévi-Strauss 1968, 229; see also 1968, 102–6).

6. In *Différence et Répetition*, Deleuze extensively examines the relationship between mind (operating by way of re-presentations and consequently through repetition) and body (in which only differences exist). Remaining true to Nietzsche, he argues that thought is nothing more than a falsifying intervention in which the empirical differences are subordinated to representational utterances of language: "the prefix Re- in the word representation signifies that conceptual form of the identi-

cal, which makes itself dependent upon the differences (Deleuze 1968, 79; English translation by Jo Smets). [le préfixe Re- dans le mot représentation signifie cette forme conceptuelle de l'identique qui se subordonne les differences.] In other words, repetition and regularity always have an idealistic connotation. It is no coincidence that Plato, presenting his theory of forms (ideas), calls the eternal the Aion.

7. At first sight, Bakhtin is not concerned with the mythical connotations of the chronotope concept. Nevertheless, keeping in mind Bakhtin's affinity with Ernst Cassirer's philosophy of culture (Brandist 2002, 98; Poole 1998), we need not be surprised if some connotations of the concept of chronotope should correlate with Cassirer's take on the mythological aspects of human experience—an experience that he defines by pointing to humanity's emotional reaction to the world. In the mythical attitude, the world appears as saturated with emotional qualities. Cassirer's philosophy of the symbolic forms distinguishes an elementary level that is associated with the mythical, with a "sympathy of the whole": "Myth and primitive religion are by no means entirely incoherent, they are not bereft of sense or reason. But their coherence depends much more upon unity of feeling" (1970, 89). In that sense, myths do not belong to a remote past, but constitute an experiential given that informs culture—even modern culture. "Even in the life of civilized man," Cassirer says, myth "has by no means lost its original power" (1970, 89).

8. The predictable is of essential importance to the conflict chronotope. Moreover, it is one of the laws of storytelling. "Suspense," says Cawelti, "is essentially the writer's ability to evoke in us a temporary sense of fear and uncertainty about the fate of a character we care about" (1976, 17).

9. Herman Pleij stresses that stories about the land of plenty are thematically linked to harmony: "the source of rejuvenescence, a continuous spring climate, absolute harmony without hate or envy and ever-present music and dancing" (1997, 93; English translation by Jo Smets). [de verjongingsbron, een permanent lenteklimaat, volslagen harmonie zonder haat of nijd en altijd muziek en dansen.]

10. Apart from heterotopias embodying ideal situations, Foucault mentions "crisis heterotopias" (that is, "privileged or sacred or forbidden places, reserved for individuals who are, in relation to society and to the human environment in which they live, in a state of crisis: adolescents, menstruating women, pregnant women, the elderly, etc."; Foucault 1986, 24) and bourgeois-modern "heterotopias of deviation" ("those in which individuals whose behavior is deviant in relation to the required mean or norm are placed. Cases of this are rest homes and psychiatric hospitals, and of course prison"; Foucault 1986, 25).

11. Foucault emphasizes the interweaving of time and space: "the fatal intersection of time with space" (1986, 22). The feature of heterochrony is also inherent to the definition of heterotopy: "the heterotopia begins to function at full capacity when men arrive at a sort of absolute break with their traditional time" (Foucault 1986, 26).

12. In this sense, my applying the name "Aion" as a concept of time differs from other usages. Deleuze and Guattari, for example, use the same concept to denote the very opposite meaning: "floating, nonpulsed time proper to Aeon, in other words, the time of the pure event or of becoming" (Deleuze and Guattari 2004, 263 and 1980, 322). [le temps non pulse flottant proper à l'Aiôn, c'est-à-dire le temps de l'événement pur ou du devenir.] The opposition is easy to explain. Since *Différence et Répétition*, Deleuze is trying to redefine "repetition" by contrasting it with habits and general ideas (to which the concept usually applies). Although I may have a philosophical affinity with the idea of repetition as "becoming," as "repetition of the same in something different," in this study I use the concept in the meaning that is challenged by Deleuze.

13. These kinds of worldviews, however, do not only concern time. Behind the absolute regularity and repetition, an absolutized concept of space is also hidden. Aristotle, followed by Plotinus, was the first to conceive space as an unchanging structure in which regular processes gradually unfold. A similar balance chronotope lies at the basis of a problem Isaac Newton struggled with in natural science. An implication of his newly found laws was that there was no such thing as absolute space, yet for metaphysical reasons, Newton could not accept that objects would not have a position that could be determined with absolute certainty. Apart from the relativizing view on time already formulated by Newton, it was not until Einstein came up with a new worldview that the attention for views on relative spaces increased.

14. "Therefore, the fantastic in folklore is a *realistic* fantastic: in no way does it exceed the limits of the real, here-and-now material world, and it does not stitch together rents in that world with anything that is idealistic or other-worldly; . . . such a fantastic relies on the real-life possibilities of human development" (Bakhtin 1981a, 150; Bakhtin's emphasis).

15. In most cases, happiness, the state of *being* happy, designates an absence of conflict. When a "goal-directed plan" (see David Herman's definition of "action") succeeds and no conflicts arise from executing this plan, we can speak of a state of happiness. This also holds for the absence of conflicts in the plan a person imagines (intends) to be his or her "life plan." A variant of this is found in the definition of happiness as the absence of chance or pure luck, as *"having* luck." When fate (chance) is favorable to a person, the term "happiness" is equally applied. Conflict and chance will form a basis for defining the conflict chronotope.

16. "Folkloric time and the ancient matrices are perceived here as . . . the lost ideal of human life" (Bakhtin 1981a, 230).

17. It is possible to deduce the plausibility of Bakhtin's sketch of evolution from the urban images that were very popular in the eighteenth century. In the sentimental novel—Bakhtin associates this with the tradition of idylls—idyllic urban images can indeed be found (see Weisgerber 1978, Watt 1957, Keunen 2000).

18. Nearly all intertextual scripts mentioned by Eco can be arranged under the adventure story chronotopes: the image of a pursuit in a gothic castle or other images of the damsel in distress motif, the motif of the duel proven to be indispensable in westerns and popular fantasy stories (*Star Wars*).

19. These spaces certainly are action-spaces because they connect "a particular space (the threshold)" with "a particular time (a change)" (Collington 2006, 66; English translation by Jo Smets). [un espace particulier (le seuil) met un temps particulier (un changement).]

20. In *Le mythe de l'éternel retour* (*The Myth of the Eternal Return*), Mircea Eliade discusses the sacred time that supersedes human history and is by definition circular. The opposite of the sacred, circular, or superindividual time is the time of the individual human being, the historical time with its contingencies and unique events. This time is linear and ruled by chance. The modern human mortal, says Eliade, attaches exceptional importance to the representation of time as a linear line (1954, 152).

21. "Het Woord is niet alleen uit God geboren, zoals ook de neoplatonici zeggen, maar is ook mens geworden: en daardoor heeft de onveranderlijke God de tijd geassumeerd; daardoor is een gans andere verhouding ontstaan tussen tijd en eeuwigheid en kan men waarachtig doorheen de eerste naar de laatste gaan" (English translation by Jo Smets).

22. "The capital point (caput) of this religion is history (historia) and the prophecy of the way in which the divine providence operates in time in view of the salvation of the human race that needs to be reformed and renewed in preparation of eternal life" (Augustine quoted in De Ley 2005, *De Vera Religione*, VII: 13; English translation by Jo Smets).

23. "Damit ihm auch wirklich zu-fällt, was ihm zu-kommt, begibt der Protagonist des Artusromans sich auf die Suche nach der *aventure—adventura*. . . . Die queste des höfischen Ritters integriert im Abenteuer den Zufall in einen universalgeschichtlichen Kontext, der sich in den Gralromanen zur ritterlichen eschatologie steigert" (English translation by Jo Smets).

24. Within the group of teleologically structured narratives, an opposition can be observed between idealistic narratives (which generate a mission chronotope by means of an idealistic view of conflict chronotopes), on the one hand, and "realistic" narratives (in which the alternative view of conflict leads to a regeneration chronotope), on the other hand. The degradation chronotopes appearing in tragedy will apply to both views (for example, the idealistic view in *Oedipus Rex* and the realistic view in *Othello*).

25. In the process of cultural modernization called the Renaissance, it can be observed that this repressed or subdued culture starts claiming its rights. Certainly in literature there are noticeable changes. The narrative imagination becomes richer and leaves aside the dogmatic worldview of Christian metaphysics.

Rabelais, for example, shows the renewed power of what Bakhtin called the "folk-lore chronotope." For Bakhtin, this chronotope represents a model for the modern worldview. It is folkloric in the sense that it falls back on habits that reign supreme not among the elite, but among the rural folk and in urban trade circles. The medieval space may have been spiritual, yet the alternative conception of space is of a wordly kind; it expresses "the completely restricted, universal chronotope of human life" (Bakhtin 1981a, 242).

26. Parallel to this development runs a preference for descriptive passages in novels. This also points to a tendency to disconnect the conflict chronotope from the morally absolute, which characterizes conflict chronotopes in teleological narratives (a morality described in the third chapter). It is the case in naturalism, giving rise to a conflict chronotope that I have elsewhere called a *documentary chronotope* (Keunen 2000). The concept receives a narratological foundation (and is refined by way of justified qualifications) in Borghart 2006.

27. "Im Wirklichen die Signale des Notwendigen zu entziffern. Wahrscheinlichkeit hat aufgehört, für sinnvolle Notwendigket zu bürgen. Teleologie, auch die der nüchtern Rationalität, wird eitel Wahn angesichts der Omnipräsenz des Möglichen, die alles offen lässt für den arbiträren Zufall" (English translation by Jo Smets).

28. It is remarkable that Bakhtin casually defines the conflict chronotope. The nonutopian and nonrealistic forms of the equilibrium chronotope are identified to such an extent with the Renaissance mentality that he even describes the spatial coordinates of conflict chronotopes in terms of the "ancient matrix." The expression "familiar territory" is a clear indication of this. It is the same term he uses in his typology of the idyll (Bakhtin 1981a, 225). In any case, it would be wrong to argue that "the road" in the realistic novel constitutes a familiar environment with the same meaning as the idyll. The difficulties faced by the picaresque hero, for example, are simply irreconcilable with the notion of regularity and repetition. The road cannot be thematically arranged in the category of Hestia; instead, it must be associated with the space of a conflict chronotope—with Hermes. Hence, it would be better to substitute the term "familiar territory" with "the territory of everday encounters."

29. "S'ils font couple, pour la conscience religieuse des Grecs, c'est que les deux divinités se situent sur un même plan, que leur action s'applique au même domaine du réel, qu'ils assument des fonctions connexes. Or, au sujet d'Hestia, pas de doute possible: sa signification est transparente, son rôle strictement défini. Parce que son lot est de trôner, à jamais immobile, au centre de l'espace domestique, Hestia implique, en solidarité et contraste avec elle, le dieu véloce qui règne sur l'étendue du voyageur. À Hestia, le dedans, le clos, le fixe, le repli du groupe humain sur lui-même; à Hermès, le dehors, l'ouverture, la mobilité, le contact avec l'autre que soi" (English translation by Jo Smets).

30. "On peut dire que le couple Hermès-Hestia exprime, dans sa polarité, la tension qui se marque dans la représentation archaïque de l'espace: l'espace exige un centre, un point fixe, à valeur privilégiée, à partir duquel on puisse orienter et définir des directions, toutes différentes qualitativement; mais l'espace se présente en même temps comme lieu du mouvement, ce qui implique une possibilité de transition et de passage de n'importe quel point à un autre" (English translation by Jo Smets).

31. In a recent study, Fludernik says that "we are all tempted to see time as an objective, measurable and unambiguous category that can be pictured as a dotted line progressing from past to future" (2003, 119).

32. The "adventure novel of ordeal" is "the most widespread sub-category of the novel in European literature. It encompasses a considerable majority of all novels produced" (Bakhtin 1986, 11).

33. In his study of Dostoevsky Bakhtin focuses on the role of the character's discourse in the modern novel (he talks about the presence of *skaz*, representational and informative discourses in the story). As seen from the perspective of the study of chronotopes, other elements in Dostoevsky's work equally point to his break away from old techniques of storytelling. It appears, however, similar elements can already be detected in the work of Renaissance novelists such as Rabelais and Cervantes, and in some ways also in the classical epic and tragedy.

34. Brooks, despite being an advocate of a teleological reading of stories, argues that in the process of reading stories the tension is built up by means of the tensions between characters who are "the motor forces that drive the text forward, of the desires that connect narrative ends and beginnings, and make of the textual middle a highly charged field of force" (1984, xiii–xiv).

35. Shusterman notes how lucidly James could talk about the new method: "Yet James realized, with brave honesty, that the basic principle of drama nonetheless held the key to artistic greatness. Distinguishing nicely between the terms 'theatre-stuff' and 'drama-stuff,' between concrete stage performance and what he called the deeper 'divine principle of the Scenario' (equally realizable in novels, films, and televison), James turned that essential dramatic principle more consciously to work in composing the later works of fiction that crown his great career: 'The scenic method,' he wrote, 'is my absolute, my imperative, my *only* salvation'" (2001, 363).

36. In narratives generating teleological chronotopes, heroes are portrayed in an opposite way: "In the majority of subcategories of the novel, the plot, composition and entire internal structure of the novel postulate this unchanging nature, this solidity of the hero's image, this static nature of his unity. The hero is a constant in the novel's formula and all other quantities—the spatial environment, social position, fortune, in brief, all aspects of the hero's life and destiny—can therefore be variables" (Bakhtin 1986, 21).

37. The theologian Paul Tillich calls kairos "the moment of crisis" and "the fate of time" (Kermode 1968, 47). In a theological-eschatological view, the kairos moments relate to the final moment. Kermode explains the dualist interpretation of this pluralist concept as follows: "the End changes all, and produces, in what in relation to it is the past, these seasons, kairoi, historical moments of intemporal significance. The divine plot is the pattern of kairoi in relation to the End" (Kermode 1968, 47).

38. "«*Chronos estin en ô Kairos, Kairos d'en ô chronos ou polys*»: le temps est désormais ce dans quoi il y a Kairos (opportunité d'agir, instant propice et laps de crise) et le Kairos est ce dans quoi il n'y a pas beaucoup de temps" (English translation by Jo Smets).

39. Brooks also acknowledges that modern literature is mainly appreciated because of its characters' peripeteias being independent of the eschaton: "If at the end of a narrative we can suspend time in a moment when past and present hold together in a metaphor—which may be that recognition or anagnorisis which, said Aristotle, every good plot should bring—that moment does not abolish the movement, the slidings, the mistakes, and partial recognitions of the middle" (1984, 92).

40. In this text, however, Lotman firmly holds on to the idea that characters are singular forces in more complex stories. Recent research—consider the narratology of Possible Worlds (Pavel, Dolezel, Ryan)—instead considers characters to be vessels of counteracting forces.

41. Contrary to the traditional meta-narratives of cultural history (which are thematically concerned with the continuity between different currents and periods represented as homogeneous phenomena), a genealogy is focused on finding "contingencies, and necessity; breaks and limits, and not continuity" (Deleuze and Guattari 1972, 163; English translation by Jo Smets). [contingences, et non de la nécessité; des coupures et des limites, et non de la continuïté.] A genealogical reconstruction functions in a certain way as a form of anamnesis, of memory labor, a retrospection starting from a topical problem that, more than other problems, is engrossed with meaning. The genealogist looks for relationships of tension from the past that might shed some light on the topical problem he is currently addressing.

42. Regarding geocentrism: "The spatial-temporal world of Rabelais was the newly opened cosmos of the Renaissance. It was first of all a geographically precise cultural and historical world. Later it was the whole universe illuminated by astronomy. Man can and must conquer their entire spatial and temporal world" (Bakhtin 1981a, 242). Regarding colonial expansion: "In his novel Rabelais unfolds before us, as it were, the completely unrestricted, universal chronotope of human life. And this was fully in accord with the approaching era of great geographical and astronomical discoveries" (Bakhtin 1981a, 242).

43. My interpretation of the carnivalesque in Bakhtin's work differs from Collington's. She observes an opposition between chronotope and carnival, the

former representing sedimentation (of genres, for example) and the latter, a break (polishing off generic generalizations). Collington knows that modern texts stage a "dialogue of chronotopes" (2006, 75), but she does not notice the presence on the level of plot-space of an equally deviating concept of chronotope. Hence, she is unable to connect the concept with Bakhtin's view of the dialogicity of the modern novel. Inasmuch as the modern novel generates a dialogical chronotope, it is by definition carnivalesque: it is a parody, meta-generic and polycentric. Bakhtin's remarks about the carnivalesque in Dostoevsky's and Rabelais' texts show that the two authors shared a view of time and space that differs from metaphysically inspired worldviews.

44. In this, they are joined by recent researchers. Neff argues that the novel contributes to the inclusion of perspective and liberation of "the absolute space and time established by the monological impulses inherent in all epics" (2003, 307).

45. Because temporal processes are easily expressed in spatial categories, geometrical terms are usually used for the representation of human events: the lifeline, the way of life, the cycle of life, the matrix of the processes, and so forth. In a recent study, Fludernik says, "we are all tempted to see time as an objective, measurable and unambiguous category that can be pictured as a dotted line progressing from past to future" (2003, 119).

46. Ricoeur rightly acknowledges that modern literature, interpreted in Bakhtin's sense, establishes a new form of narrative organization, even to such an extent that he sees "the emergence of a dramatical form in which space aims to eliminate time" as an undesired side effect of Bakhtin's concept of literature. (Ricoeur 1984, 184; English translation by Jo Smets). [l'émergence d'une forme *dramatique* dans laquelle l'espace tend à supplanter le temps.] The fact is that Ricoeur agrees with Bakhtin when the latter interprets modern literature from the perspective of the dialogical structure controlling discourse, thought, and self-awareness. At the same time, he considers Bakhtin's view of this principle of composition to be dangerous, wondering "whether the dialogical principle . . . is not at the same time undermining the foundation of the structure, that is to say the organizing role of the plotting" (Ricoeur 1984, 183; English translation by Jo Smets). [si le principe dialogique . . . n'est pas en train de saper en même temps la base de l'édifice, à savoir le rôle organisateur de la mise en intrigue.] As was previously shown, Ricoeur's critique is based on a misunderstanding (the dialogical novel possesses a dialogical *plot-space*). Nevertheless, it is a meaningful misunderstanding because in his reading of Bakhtin, Ricoeur unveils his own reductionist view of literature. He is indeed is unable to think of time in a non-Aristotelian way.

47. In *Physics*, Aristotle actually was one of the first to state that an absolute space is one of the evidential facts of the human epistemic capability. According to him, movement can only be conceived if it is based on a standard for a state of being at rest.

48. In *Le Bergsonisme* (1966), Deleuze defines the subjective experience to be a mixed structure in which "duration" connects with "space." Depending on the emphasis put on either duration or space, it can be said to respectively denote subjective or objective knowledge. In the former, the characteristics of duration are emphasized: "Duration presents us with purely internal succession, without any exteriority" (1966, 29; English translation by Jo Smets). [La durée pure nous présente une succession purement interne, sans extériorité]. In the latter, the emphasis is on space, "an exteriority without succession" (1966, 29; English translation by Jo Smets). [une extériorité sans succession.] The experience of time in elementary narrative forms is characterized by the mixed structure of the subjective experience and is focused on the succession in exteriority; the center of attention is not the experience of time but the staging of the spatially ordered temporal structure. In dialogical plot-spaces, however, a space is created in which simultaneity and the mutual symbiosis of time moments (and not succession) hold the central position ("an exteriority without succession").

49. In *Matière et mémoire*, Bergson states that consciousness of duration is integrally related to memory: "The 'subjectivity' of sensory qualities mainly consists in a sort of contraction of the real, operated by our memory" (1896: 184; English translation by Jo Smets). [La "subjectivité" des qualités sensibles consiste surtout dans une espèce de contraction du réelle, opérée par notre mémoire.] Kümmel generalizes the statement as follows: "It does not develop like a measurable time from homogenous, equally passing parts. Rather, it gathers its successive contents in one go in a whole, in which all alternately can pervade and thus remain present at the same time" (Kümmel 1962, 17; English translation by Jo Smets). [Sie baut sich nicht wie eine gemessene Zeit aus homogenen, gleichmäßig verfließenden Teilen auf, vielmehr sammelt sie ihre sukzedierenden Inhalte zugleich in ein Ganzes, in dem sich alle wechselseitig durchdringen und so zugleich präsent bleiben.]

50. "La durée est essentiellement mémoire, conscience, liberté. Et elle est conscience et liberté, parce qu'elle est d'abord mémoire" (English translation by Jo Smets).

51. The Bergsonian "duration" is a time which "swells as it progresses, . . . it preserves the entire past, but does not contain the future" (Prigogine 1984, 30; English translation by Jo Smets). [aanzwelt naarmate hij voortschrijdt, . . . hij bewaart het hele verleden, maar hij houdt de toekomst niet in.] It is a "successive developing of a quality inside a present" (Kümmel 1962, 17; English translation by Jo Smets). [sukzessives Aufbauen einer Qualität innerhalb einer Präsenz.]

52. "This opens up the perspective," De Ley continues by quoting Maertens (1965), "that truth can never be a ready-made teaching or doctrine only to be accepted and once and for all acquired: 'the Truth essentially is not something that we find, but something which we seek'" (Maertens 1965). (English translation by Jo Smets). [Dat opent het perspectief dat de waarheid nooit een kant-en-klare leer

of doctrine kan zijn, die men aanvaardt en eens en voor goed verwerft: "de Waarheid is essentieel niet iets dat men vindt, maar dat men zoekt."]

Chapter 3

1. The image of the homecoming is related to what was said above concerning Hestia (see Vernant). Philosophically speaking, it can be considered as the creation of an "inner world." In French philosophy, in particular in the work of Maurice Blanchot, Foucault, and Deleuze, a major part is played by the distinction between "inside" and "outside" (see Deleuze and Parnet 1977, 73). In this radically antiteleological philosophy, the evaluation of "inside" and "outside" is completely reversed.

2. In *A Pluralistic Universe*, William James sees Hegel's philosophy as an interesting solution to the problem of negativity: "What he did with the category of negation was his most original stroke. . . . [Hegel] saw that in a fashion negation also relates things; and he had the brilliant idea of transcending the ordinary logic by treating advance from the different to the different as if it were also a necessity of thought. 'The so-called maxim of identity,' he wrote, 'is supposed to be accepted by the consciousness of every one. . . . We must never view identity as abstract identity, to the exclusion of all difference. That is the touchstone for distinguishing all bad philosophy from what alone deserves the name of philosophy. If thinking were no more than registering abstract identities, it would be a most superfluous performance. Things and concepts are identical with themselves only in so far as at the same time they involve distinction'" (1909). The excerpt quoted by James perfectly expresses the opposition between myth and story: a myth operates with abstract identities that have been a priori posited; stories bring about identities in a context of difference and change. An identity arising from a process has a greater foundation in experience than identities postulated in a dogmatic fashion.

3. Lotman observes that narratives with sparse elaborations on the relationships of tension between characters are closer to mythical thought than narratives in which the negative is diffused over different points. "Looked at typologically, the initial situation is that a certain plot-space is divided by a single boundary into an internal and an external sphere, and a single character has the opportunity to cross that boundary; this situation is now replaced by a more complex derivative. . . . The more noticeably the world of the characters is reduced to singularity (one hero, one obstacle), the nearer it, is to the primordial mythological type of structural organization of the text" (Lotman 1979, 167).

4. This seemingly teleological movement from starting to final point has become the basis for certain theorists, for example, Brooks, to proceed to an absolutized vision of the teleological plot. In a sense, the term is applicable, but in my

opinion, it is better for typological reasons to reserve the term "teleological" for a dialectical-eschatological plot logic. If we start using the notion in a somewhat perfunctory fashion, the distinction between the plot development of a melodrama and that of an adventure story becomes unthinkable.

5. Let me explain this contrast with an example. A whodunit crime story seems to uncover a truth (notably the true facts of the crime case). Morally speaking, however, any disclosure is out of the question. From the start of the narrative, the punishability of the crime is firmly established and undisputed. The end, in other words, confirms the a priori given value.

6. From the opening passages of Greek creational myths, we can clearly infer that myths claim to designate the truth about the universal—usually natural—laws of the cosmos. Hesiod writes: "Verily at the first Chaos came to be, but next wide-bosomed Earth, the ever-sure foundations of all (4) the deathless ones who hold the peaks of snowy Olympus, and dim Tartarus in the depth of the wide-pathed Earth, and Eros (Love), fairest among the deathless gods, who unnerves the limbs and overcomes the mind and wise counsels of all gods and all men within them. From Chaos came forth Erebus and black Night; but of Night were born Aether (5) and Day, whom she conceived and bare from union in love with Erebus. And Earth first bare starry Heaven, equal to herself, to cover her on every side, and to be an ever-sure abiding-place for the blessed gods. And she brought forth long Hills, graceful haunts of the goddess-Nymphs who dwell amongst the glens of the hills. She bare also the fruitless deep with his raging swell, Pontus, without sweet union of love" (1914).

7. "The true character of mythical being is first revealed when it appears as the being of origins. All the sanctity of mythical being goes back ultimately to the sanctity of the origin" (Cassirer 1975, 105).

8. In *The Hero with a Thousand Faces* (1949), Joseph Campbell describes the mission chronotope in a language that aptly expresses its ritual character. In his opinion, the main movements in this chronotope are *departure, initiation,* and *return:* "A hero ventures forth from the world of common day into a region of supernatural wonder: fabulous forces are there encountered and a decisive victory is won: the hero comes back from this mysterious adventure with the power to bestow boons on his fellow man" (1968, 30).

9. It is typical of regeneration chronotopes that the equilibrium chronotopes at the beginning of the narrative give little cause for representations of ideals or pleasant things. Although sometimes a condition of equilibrium is indeed staged (the marital plans in the opening of Bram Stoker's *Dracula*), the story is, in fact, not launched until the emergence of the degraded state in which the character suddenly finds himself (the promise to Dracula to spend a few weeks in his castle). The state of equilibrium is only marginal and is accompanied neither by the hero or heroine being charged with a task nor by an exposition of his or her virtues—

Propp's idea of putting the hero to the test. In contrast to the mission chronotope, where at the start of the narrative the world is shown in all its glory, there is no clear representation of ideals, which will only be clarified when the negative chronotope is evoked, that is, as the counterpart of the negative that is shown.

10. "If the hero in his triumph wins the blessing of the goddess or the god and is then explicitly commissioned to return to the world with some elixir for the restoration of society, the final stage of his adventure is supported by all the powers of his supernatural patron. On the other hand, if the trophy has been attained against the opposition of its guardian, or if the hero's wish to return to the world has been resented by the gods or demons, then the last stage of the mythological round becomes a lively, often comical, pursuit. This flight may be complicated by marvels of magical obstruction and evasion" (Campbell 1968, 196).

11. Bakhtin states that the desire for balance strongly resembles idyllic poetry. The idyll is also the genre Frye refers to when he defines the comic mode of epics and other, more ancient forms of narrative (1973, 43).

12. Campbell adds that a heroic quest of this sort always is a quest for the "self": "The adventure of the hero represents the moment in his life when he achieved illumination—the nuclear moment when, while still alive, he found and opened the road to the light beyond the dark walls of our living death" (1968, 259).

13. In Northrop Frye's typology of narratives, epic heroes are of a similar nature as the heroes of the sacred world because they are "superior in degree to other men and to his environment" (Frye 1973, 33).

14. The hero is sacred because he discovers the timeless and the universal in the temporary and the contingent. He is the myth's keeper: "The hero, therefore, is the man or woman who has been able to battle past his personal and local historical limitations to the generally valid, normally human forms. . . . The hero has died as a modern man; but as eternal man—perfected, unspecific, universal man—he has been reborn. His second solemn task and deed therefore (as Toynbee declares and as all the mythologies of mankind indicate) is to return then to us, transfigured, and teach the lesson he has learned of life renewed" (Campbell 1968, 19–20).

15. Hence, there is the artificial tragicomic effect some tragic poets choose to add to their work. Euripides' deus ex machina mends the different parts of the narrative, enabling the narrative to end as the above-mentioned superhero stories. Comicality is never completely absent in a tragedy. To be sure, there is still tension (desire for equilibrium) because as Aristotle rightly argued, the tragedy very frequently shifts the state of equilibrium toward the spectator. Throughout the anticipation of the catharsis, the audience will never be able to forget the eschaton.

16. Hogan is correct to write that the staging of suffering is important in raising moral empathy (2004, 213). Karel Boullart, in his unsurpassed classes of philosophical aesthetics at Ghent University, similarly argues that failure and

heterotelism are inherently tied up with humanity's faculties of action (Boullart 1999, 332 and 435).

17. According to Bradley (following Aristotle's strict teachings about the plot), chance is never allowed to impede the necessity of a teleological development: "any large admission of chance into the tragic sequence would certainly weaken, and might destroy, the sense of the causal connection of character, deed, and catastrophe" (1905, 15).

18. "As a Shakespearean tragedy represents a conflict that ends in a catastrophe, any such tragedy may roughly be divided into three parts. The first of these sets forth or expounds the situation, or state of affairs, from which the conflict arises; therefore, it can be called the Exposition. The second deals with *the definite beginning, the growth and the vicissitudes of the conflict.* Accordingly, it forms *the bulk of the play,* comprising the Second, Third and Fourth Acts, and usually a part of the Fifth. The final section of the tragedy shows the issue of the conflict in a catastrophe" (Bradley 1905, 40–41; my emphasis).

19. Although it is not infrequently the case that both a seeker-hero/heroine and a victim-hero/heroine are present (in the Greek romances—the oldest adventure novels—the heroes and heroines are respectively seeker-heroes and victim-heroines), and although many heroes unite elements of both seekers and victims in themselves (the hero in the horror story is seeking his love but at the same time becomes a defenseless victim of ghosts and vampires), in most traditional texts a mission or a regeneration mode is easily detected. It is, therefore, the temporal pattern that ensures that a narrative is perceived as either a mission chronotope or a regeneration chronotope. If the narrative fails to be understood by way of a circular movement and if, in fact, only the return is described, the recipient invariably is handling a regeneration chronotope.

20. In day-to-day time, Bakhtin observes the first signs of what he calls the "historical time." In the realistic eschatology featured prominently in the regeneration chronotope, it is possible to bring up the "world of the author himself" and offer the reader recognizable views and situations (1981a, 103).

21. A fine example of this is Stoker's *Dracula*. Superficially, Harker's journey to Transylvania seems to be the beginning of a mission chronotope. A notary clerk (who has a bright future with a fiancée), Harker is charged with the task of settling an inheritance with a client in Central Europe. In this way, the meeting with Dracula is the breaking of a boundary. This development, however, is merely a secondary plot line, because the story, the primary plot line, does not start until a greater conflict appears, a greater confrontation with the negative. The secondary plot line is swiftly shown to be banal: Dracula signs the contract soon enough. It is in the course of this signing that the primary plot line is launched: the negative reveals itself in the count's demand that Harker spend a few months in his terrifying castle. At this point, the main set of dynamics is initiated, constituting the

most important change featured in *Dracula:* the virtually impossible battle with a series of conflict chronotopes (a series of pursuits, nightmares, escaped villains, confidants affected by the evil, etc.).

22. In fact, Hogan solely studies the regeneration and mission chronotopes. He divides texts from both groups in three thematic categories—the romantic comedy, the heroic comedy, and the sacrificial tragicomedy: "basically, romantic plots concern the separation and re-union of lovers. Heroic plots concern the dis-placement of the hero from his/her rightful social position, a threat to the hero's society, and the hero's defense of that society against the threat. Sacrificial plots concern the devastation of a society and the restoration of communal well-being through sacrifice" (Hogan 2003).

23. It could be argued that the interiorized conflicts and equilibriums are typi-cal for all texts with powerfully elaborated psychological themes. The oldest forms of psychological conflicts in world literature are found in the *Iliad.* An interiorized conflict is even at the core of Homer's work: Achilles' grudge.

24. It is, however, possible that apart from a dialogical plot-space, a narrative also develops a storyline that is tied to a teleological representation. As was said before, apart from a network of relationships of tension, many modern novels also contain a simpler storylines, such as a crime plot (mission chronotope) or a love plot (regeneration chronotope).

25. Historically speaking, the designation "tragicomedy" refers to eighteenth-century bourgeois comedies (*comédie larmoyante,* Restoration comedy, comedy of manners) that aspired to the earnestness of canonized pieces from the past (almost invariably tragedies). On closer analysis, these pieces are often shown to have a tele-ological plot (regeneration and mission chronotopes, in particular, are frequent)—just like the melodramas of the boulevard theater studied by Brooks. Modern dramas, by contrast, focus their attention more on the design of a dialogical chronotope because of their keen interest in sociological and psychoanalytical conflicts.

26. The anagnorisis is the moment in which the tragic action reaches its cul-minating point: the characters (and the protagonist, in particular) learn the truth of their actions and draw their conclusions. The disclosure not only implies the truth but also the recognition of—the consciousness-awakening to—the real facts of the case. This combination of disclosure and recognition results in the well-known tragic effect: the emotion of grief and the catastrophic insight that an innocent human being suffers from a situation for which he or she carries no guilt. For ex-ample, Oedipus arrives at the turnabout point of his life story when the Corinthian messenger reveals to him that his real father is not Polybus but Laius. Thanks to this anagnorisis, Oedipus realizes and knows that he arrived involuntarily at the disgraceful situation pointed out to him by the oracle.

27. During the moment of agnition, a form of "dramatic irony" emerges: the character is unaware of a specific state of things (he or she does not know the

important facts or interprets them incorrectly), and this results in a relationship of tension with the recipient's state of consciousness—the recipient being well aware of the full facts of the case (just as the audience is in a tragedy). The moment at which the character's (subjective) perspective begins to converge with the neutral or objective perspective of the recipient, the moment in which both have grasped the real truth, is exactly the moment in which the differences in tragic and comic forms of the dialogical chronotope are at their most visible.

28. This, in fact, is the difference between classical and modern tragedy. Whereas the former, if we take Aristotle's word for it, equally aspires to a process of disclosure, in modern tragedy this process will unfold without anyone distinctly knowing what is being veiled or disclosed. Othello's problem is not his blindness with regard to the will of the gods and moral law, but his lack of insight in the mechanisms of blind passions.

29. "The form of the idyll assumed great significance in the 18th century, when the problem of time in literature was posed with particular intensity, a period when precisely a new feeling for time was beginning to awake. One is struck by the wealth and variety of types of idylls in the 18th century. . . . The problem of time is elevated to the level of philosophy in several 18th century idylls. The real organic time of idyllic life is opposed to the frivolous, fragmented time of city life or even to historical time" (Bakhtin 1981a, 228).

30. As was indicated above, a Hegelian line of reasoning needs to fulfill the conditions of the idealistic eschatology, while a Hegelian plot course corresponds best with a mission chronotope. Moretti refers to the derivative of the Hegelian circle, the movement of "return," typical of regeneration chronotopes.

31. Comic forms of agnition also characterize the bourgeois melodrama, first gaining popularity in drama (the eighteenth-century *comédies des moeurs* and the op- era librettos of Lorenzo da Ponte), then in the novel (the sentimental melodramas of Dickens or Harriet Beecher Stowe and the adventurous melodramas of Walter Scott). Even though the hero or heroine often emerges from a fight a little the worse for wear, and even though the initial equilibrium seems profoundly dis- turbed, he or she will discover the seeds of a new equilibrium at the end (a new partner, a new world with social reforms, a stronger spiritual belief, the prospect of a glorious future).

32. My references to Shakespeare's *Othello* already indicated that, in theater, tragic forms of the dialogical chronotope are also a phenomenon of modernity.

33. In this sense, Judith Butler has called the modern novel's hero "Hegel's unhappy hero." Heroes refusing the "comfort of civilisation" are frustrated heroes: "before mediated self-reflection is achieved, the subject knows itself to be a more limited, less autonomous being than it potentially is" (Butler 1987, 8).

Works Cited

Alquié, Ferdinand. 1939. *Leçons de philosophie: Psychologie.* Toulouse: Didier.

Anderson, J. R. 1980. *Cognitive Psychology and Its Implications.* San Francisco: Freeman.

Aristotle. 1929. *Poetics.* Trans. S. H. Butcher. London: Macmillan. The Internet Classics Archive. http://classics.mit.edu//Aristotle/poetics.html (accessed April 24, 2010).

Attebery, Brian. 1992. *Strategies of Fantasy.* Bloomington: Indiana University Press.

Bakhtin, Mikhail M. 1981a. "Forms of Time and of the Chronotope in the Novel: Notes Toward a Historical Poetics." In *The Dialogic Imagination,* ed. Michael Holquist, trans. Caryl Emerson and Michael Holquist, 84–254. Austin: University of Texas Press.

———. 1981b. "Epos and the Novel." In *The Dialogic Imagination,* ed. Michael Holquist, trans. Caryl Emerson and Michael Holquist, 1–83. Austin: University of Texas Press.

———. 1984a. *Problems of Dostoevsky's Poetics.* ed. and trans. Caryl Emerson. Manchester: Manchester University Press. (Orig. pub. 1929.)

———. 1984b. *Rabelais and His World.* Trans. Helene Iswolsky. Bloomington: Indiana University Press. (Orig. pub. 1965.)

———. 1986. "The Bildungsroman and Its Significance in the History of Realism." In *Speech Genres and Other Late Essays,* ed. Caryl Emerson and Michael Holquist, 10–59. Austin: University of Texas Press.

Bal, Mieke. 1978. *De theorie van vertellen en verhalen: Inleiding in de narratologie.* Muiderberg: Coutinho.

Barthes, Roland. 1970. *S/Z.* Paris: Seuil.

———. 1975. *The Pleasure of the Text.* New York: Hill and Wang. (Orig. pub. 1973.)

Bartlett, Frederic C. 1967. *Remembering: A Study in Experimental and Social Psychology.* Cambridge: Cambridge University Press. (Orig. pub. 1932.)

Beer, Gillian. 1983. *Darwin's Plot: Evolutionary Narrative in Darwin, George Eliot, and Nineteenth-Century Fiction.* London: Routledge.

Bemong, Nele, Pieter Borghart, Michel De Dobbeleer, Kristoffel Demoen, Koen De Temmerman, and Bart Keunen, eds. 2010. *Bakhtin's Theory of the Literary Chronotope: Reflections, Applications, Perspectives.* Ghent: Academia Press.

Bergson, Henri. 1959. "Matière et mémoire: Essai sur la relation du corps à l'esprit." In *Oeuvres,* ed. André Robinet, 161–382. Paris: PUF. (Orig. pub. 1896.)

Booker, Christopher. 2004. *The Seven Basic Plots: Why We Tell Stories*. London: Continuum.

Borges, Jorge Luis. 1998. "The Babel Lottery." In *Collected Fictions*, trans. Andrew Hurley, 101–6. New York: Penguin Putnam. (Orig. pub. 1941.)

Borghart, Pieter. 2006. *De narratologische code(s) van het Europese naturalisme*. Ghent: Academia Press.

Boullart, Karel. 1999. *Vanuit Andromeda gezien: Het bereikbare en het toegankelijke*. Brussels: VUB Press.

Bradley, A. C. 1905. *Shakespearean Tragedy: Lectures on Hamlet, Othello, King Lear, Macbeth*. London: Macmillan.

Brandist, Craig. 2002. *The Bakhtin Circle: Philosophy, Culture and Politics*. London: Pluto Press.

Bremond, Claude. 1981. "La logique des possibles narratifs." In *L'analyse structurale du récit (Communications 8)*, ed. Roland Barthes et al., 66–83. Paris: Seuil. (Orig. pub. 1966.)

Brooks, Peter. 1984. *Reading for the Plot: Design and Intention in Narrative*. New York: Vintage.

———. 1995. *The Melodramatic Imagination: Balzac, Henry James, Melodrama, and the Mode of Excess*. New Haven, Conn.: Yale University Press. (Orig. pub. 1976.)

Bruner, Jerome. 1986. *Actual Minds, Possible Worlds*. Cambridge, Mass.: Harvard University Press.

———. 1991. "The Narrative Construction of Reality." *Critical Inquiry* 18 (1): 1–21.

Buchloh, Paul, ed. 1973. *Der Detektivroman: Studien zur Geschichte und Form der englischen und amerikanischen Detektivliteratur*. Darmstadt: Wissenschaftliche Buchgesellschaft.

Butler, Judith. 1984. *Subjects of Desire: Hegelian Reflections in Twentieth-Century France*. New York: Columbia University Press.

Campbell, Joseph. 1968. *The Hero with a Thousand Faces*. Princeton, N.J.: Princeton University Press. (Orig. pub. 1949.)

Cassirer, Ernst. 1970. *An Essay on Man*. New York: Bantam. (Orig. pub. 1944.)

———. 1975. *The Philosophy of Symbolic Forms*. Vol. 2 of *Mythical Thought*. New Haven, Conn.: Yale University Press. (Orig. pub. 1925.)

Castoriadis, Cornelius. 1975. *L'institution imaginaire de la société*. Paris: Seuil.

Cawelti, John. 1976. *Adventure, Mystery, and Romance: Formula Stories as Art and Popular Culture*. Chicago: University of Chicago Press.

Chrétien De Troyes. 1914. "Lancelot or, the Knight of the Cart." *Chrétien De Troyes: Arthurian Romances*. Trans. W. W. Comfort. London: Everyman's Library. http://omacl.org/Lancelot/ (accessed April 24, 2010; written ca. 1180).

Collington, Tara. 2006. *Lectures chronotopiques: Espace, temps et genres romanesques*. Montreal: XYZ.

Coplan, Amy. 2004. "Empathic Engagement with Narrative Fictions." *Journal of Aesthetics and Art Criticism* 2:141–52.

Crane, Ronald. 2002. "The Concept of Plot and the Plot of *Tom Jones*." In *Narrative Dynamics: Essays on Time, Plot, Closure, and Frames*, ed. Brian Richardson, 94–101. Columbus: Ohio State University Press.

Deleuze, Gilles. 1966. *Le Bergsonisme*. Paris: PUF.

———. 1968. *Différence et répetition*. Paris: PUF.

———. 1986. *Cinema 1: The mouvement-image*. London: Athlone Press. (Orig. pub. 1983.)

Deleuze, Gilles, and Félix Guattari. 1972. *Capitalisme et schizophrénie 1: L' Anti-Oedipe*. Paris: Minuit.

———. 1980. *Capitalisme et Schizophrénie 2: Mille Plateaux*. Paris: Minuit.

———. 2004. *Capitalism and Schizophrenia 2: A Thousand Plateaus*. Trans. Brian Massumi. London and New York: Continuum. (Orig. pub. 1980.)

Deleuze, Gilles, and Claire Parnet. 1977. *Dialogues*. Paris: Flammarion.

De Ley, Herman. 2007. *Antieke Wijsbegeerte van Thales tot Augustinus: Een syllabus*. http://www.flwi.ugent.be/cie/1ba/augustinus.html/ (accessed April 24, 2010).

Denis, Michael. 1991. *Image and Cognition*. New York: Harvester. (Orig. pub. 1989.)

Dolezel, Lubomir. 1979. "Extensional and Intensional Narrative Worlds." *Poetics Today* 1:7–25.

Eco, Umberto. 1988. *De Structuur van de slechte smaak*. Amsterdam: Bert Bakker.

———. 1989. *Lector in fabula: De rol van de lezer in narratieve teksten*. Amsterdam: Bert Bakker. (Orig. pub. 1979.)

Eliade, Mircea. 1954. *Cosmos and History: The Myth of the Eternal Return*. Trans. W. R. Trask. Princeton, N.J.: Princeton University Press.

Elias, Norbert. 1985. *Een essay over tijd*. Meulenhoff: Amsterdam. (Orig. pub. 1974.)

Farvardyn Project. 2010. "The God of Infinite Time." In *An Illustrated Reference Portal on Ancient Persia*. http://www.farvardyn.com/mithras5.php/ (accessed April 28, 2010).

Fleming, Ian. 1960. *For Your Eyes Only: Five Secret Occasions in the Life of James Bond*. London: Jonathan Cape.

———. 1965. *The Man with the Golden Gun*. New York: New American Library of World Literature.

Fludernik, Monika. 2003. "Chronology, Time, Tense and Experientiality in Narrative." *Language and Literature* 12 (2): 117–34.

Foucault, Michel. 1986. "Of Other Spaces." *Diacritics* 16 (1): 22–27.

Frank, Erich. 1975. "Die Bedeutung der Geschichte für das christliche Denkens." In *Zum Augustinus-Gespräch der Gegenwart*, ed. Carl Andresen, 381–96. Darmstadt: Wissenschaftlichen Buchgesellschaft. (Orig. pub. 1955.)

Friedman, Norman. 1955. "Forms of the Plot." *Journal of General Education* 8: 241–53

Frye, Northrop. 1973. *Anatomy of Criticism: Four Essays.* Princeton, N.J.: Princeton University Press. (Orig. pub. 1957.)

Garland, David. 1990. "Frameworks of Inquiry in the Sociology of Punishment." *British Journal of Sociology* 41 (1): 1–15.

Gaut, Berys. 1999. "Identification and Emotion in Narrative Fiction." In *Passionate Views: Film, Cognition, and Emotion,* ed. Carl Plantinga and Greg M. Smith, 200–216. Baltimore: Johns Hopkins University Press.

Greimas, Algirdas Julien. 1966. *Sémantique structural.* Paris: Larousse.

———. 1981. "Eléments pour une théorie de l'interprétation du récit mythique." In *L'analyse structurale du récit (Communications 8),* ed. Roland Barthes et al., 34–65. Paris: Seuil. (Orig. pub. 1966.)

Hawking, Stephen, and Leonard Mlodinov. 2005. *Een korte geschiedenis van de tijd.* Amsterdam: Bert Bakker.

Hegel, G. W. F. 1837. *The Philosophy of History.* Trans. J. Sibree. Online text by Carl Mickelsen. http://www.class.uidaho.edu/mickelsen/texts/Hegel%20-%20 Philosophy%20of%20History.htm/ (accessed April 26, 2010).

———. 1993. *Introductory Lectures on Aesthetics.* Trans. Bernard Bosanquet. London: Penguin. (Orig. pub. 1835–38.)

Herman, David. 2002. *Story Logic: Problems and Possibilities of Narrative.* Lincoln and London: University of Nebraska Press.

———. 2005. "Conflict." In *The Routledge Encyclopedia of Narrative Theory,* ed. David Herman, Manfred Jahn, and Marie-Laure Ryan, 83. London: Routledge.

Herman, Luc, and Bart Vervaeck. 2005. *Handbook of Narrative Analysis.* Lincoln and London: University of Nebraska Press.

Hesiod. 1914. *The Theogony.* http://www.sacred-texts.com/cla/hesiod/theogony .htm/ (accessed April 26, 2010).

Hillebrand, Bruno. 1971. "Poetischer, philosophischer, mathematischer Raum." In *Landschaft und Raum in der Erzählkunst,* ed. A. Ritter, 417–64. Darmstadt: Wissenschaftlichte Buchgesellschaft.

Hogan, Patrick Colm. 2003. *Literary Universals.* http://litup.unipa.it/docs/story .htm/ (accessed April 26, 2010).

———. 2004. *The Mind and Its Stories.* Cambridge: Cambridge University Press.

Holquist, Michael. 1990. *Dialogism: Bakhtin and His World.* London: Routledge.

Jahn, Manfred. 2005. *Narratology: A Guide to the Theory of Narrative.* http://www .uni-koeln.de/~ame02/pppn.htm/ (version 1.8. 28 May 2005; accessed January 2, 2006).

James, Henry. 1884. "The Art of Fiction." *Longman's Magazine* 4. http://guweb2 .gonzaga.edu/faculty/campbell/engl462/artfiction.html/ (accessed April 26, 2010).

———. 1908. *What Maisie Knew.* http://www2.newpaltz.edu/~hathawar/maisie1 .html/ (accessed April 26, 2010). (Orig. pub. 1897.)

———. 2001. Preface. *The Portrait of a Lady.* Project Gutenberg. http://www.gutenberg
.org/etext/2833/ (accessed April 26, 2010). (Orig. pub. 1881; online version
orig. pub. 1908.)

James, William. 1996. *Varieties of Religious Experience: A Study in Human Nature.* Project
Gutenberg. http://www.gutenberg.org/etext/621/ (accessed April 26, 2010).
(Orig. pub. 1902.)

———. 2004. *A Pluralistic Universe: Hibbert Lectures at Manchester College on the Present
Situation in Philosophy.* Project Gutenberg. http://www.gutenberg.org/etext/
11984/ (accessed April 26, 2010). (Orig. pub. 1909.)

Kermode, Frank. 1968. *The Sense of an Ending: Studies in the Theory of Fiction.* London:
Oxford University Press. (Orig. pub. 1966.)

Keunen, Bart. 2000a. *De verbeelding van de grootstad: Stads- en wereldbeelden in het proza van
de moderniteit.* Brussel: VUB Press.

———. 2000b. "Bakhtin, Genre Formation and the Cognitive Turn: Chronotopes
as Memory Schemata." *CLCWeb: Comparative Literature and Culture: A WWWeb
Journal* 2:2 (June). http://clcwebjournal.lib.purdue.edu/clcweb00-2/keunen00
.html/ (accessed April 26, 2010).

———. 2005. *Tijd voor een verhaal: Mens- en wereldbeelden in de (populaire) verhaalcultuur.*
Ghent: Academia Press.

King, Stephen. 1977. *The Shining.* Garden City, N.Y.: Doubleday.

King James Bible. http://bible.gospelcom.net/ (accessed April 26, 2010).

Klotz, Volker. 1979. *Abenteuer-Romane: Sue, Dumas, Ferry, Retcliffe, May, Verne.* Munich:
Hanser.

Köhler, Erich. 1973. *Der literarische Zufall. Das Mögliche und die Notwendigkeit.* Munich:
Fink.

Könönen, Maija. 2003. *"Four Ways of Writing the City": St. Petersburg-Leningrad as a
Metaphor in the Poetry of Joseph Brodsky.* Helsinki: Helsinki University Press.

Kümmel, Friedrich. 1962. *Ueber den Begriff der Zeit.* Tübingen: Niemeyer. http://
friedrich-kuemmel.de/zeit.html/ (accessed April 26, 2010).

Ladin, Jay. 1999. "Fleshing Out the Chronotope." In *Critical Essays on Mikhail Bakhtin,*
ed. Caryl Emerson, 212–36. New York: Hall.

Lotman, Jurij. M. 1977. *The Structure of the Artistic Text.* Trans. Gail Lenhoff and Ronald Vroon. Ann Arbor: University of Michigan. (Orig. pub. 1970.)

———. 1979. "The Origin of Plot in the Light of Typology." *Poetics Today* 1 (1/2):
161–84. (Orig. pub. 1973.)

———. 1981. "Text Within Text." *Soviet Psychology* 26 (3): 32–51. (Orig. pub.
1972.)

———. 1990. *Universe of the Mind: A Semiotic Theory of Culture.* Trans. Ann Shukman.
London: Tauris.

Lüthi, Max. 1976. *Once upon a Time: On the Nature of Fairy Tales.* Bloomington: Indiana
University Press.

Maertens, Georges. 1965. "Augustinus over de mens: Een visie op de menselijke in-
nerlijkheid tussen hellenisme en christendom." *Verhandelingen van de Koninklijke
Vlaamse Academie voor Wetenschap, Letteren en Schone Kunsten* 54:112–20.

Maingueneau, Dominique. 1997. *Pragmatique pour le discours littéraire.* Paris: Dunod.
(Orig. pub. 1990.)

Medvedev, Pavel N., and Mikhail M. Bakhtin. 1978. *The Formal Method in Literary
Scholarship: A Critical Introduction to Sociological Poetics.* Trans. A. J. Wehrle. Baltimore: Johns Hopkins University Press. (Orig. pub. 1928.)

Meutsch, Dietrich. 1986. "Mental Models in Literary Discourse: Towards the
Integration of Linguistic and Psychological Levels of Description." *Poetics*
15:307–31.

Meyer, Helmut. 1971. "Raumgestaltung und Raumsymbolik in der Erzählkunst."
In *Landschaft und Raum in der Erzählkunst,* ed. A. Ritter, 208–31. Darmstadt: Wissenschaftlichte Buchgesellschaft. (Orig. pub. 1957.)

Miller, Stuart. 1967. *The Picaresque Novel.* Cleveland, Ohio: Press of Case Western
Reserve University.

Minsky, Marvin. 1975. "A Framework for Representing Knowledge." In *The Psychology of Computer Vision,* ed. Patrick Winston, 211–77. New York: McGraw-
Hill.

Mitterand, Henri. 1990. *Zola: L'histoire et la fiction.* Paris: PUF.

Modledski, Tania. 1982. *Loving with a Vengeance: Mass-Produced Fantasies for Women.*
New York: Methuen.

Moretti, Franco. 1983. *Signs Taken as Wonders: Essays in the Sociology of Literary Forms.*
London: Verso.

———. 1987. *The Way of the World: The Bildungsroman in European Culture.* London:
Verso.

Mori, Masaki. 1997. *Epic Grandeur: Toward a Comparative Poetics of the Epic.* Albany:
State University of New York Press.

Morris, Pam, ed. 1994. *The Bakhtin Reader.* London: Edward Arnold.

Morson, Gary Saul. 1991. "Bakhtin, Genres and Temporality." *New Literary History*
22:1071–92.

Morson, Gary Saul, and Caryl Emerson. 1990. *Mikhail Bakhtin: Creation of a Prosaic.*
Stanford, Calif.: Stanford University Press.

Neff, David Sprague. 2003. "Into the Heart of the Heart of the Chronotope: Dialogism, Theoretical Physics, and Catastrophe Theory." In *Mikhail Bakhtin,* ed.
Michael E. Gardiner, 304–20. London: Sage.

Neill, Alex. 1996. "Empathy and (Film) Fiction." In *Post-theory: Reconstructing Film
Studies,* ed. David Bordwell and Noël Carroll, 175–94. Madison: University
of Wisconsin Press.

Nell, Victor. 1988 *Lost in a Book: The Psychology of Reading for Pleasure.* New Haven,
Conn.: Yale University Press.

Nietzsche, Friedrich. 1878. *Human, All Too Human.* Trans. Helen Zimmern. http:// users.compaqnet.be/cn127103/Nietzsche_human_all_too_human/sect2 _on_the_History_of_Moral_Feelings.htm/ (accessed April 26, 2010).

———. 2001. *The Gay Science.* Trans. Josefine Nauckhoff and Adrian Del Caro. Cambridge: Cambridge University Press. (Orig. pub. 1882.)

Nusser, Peter. 1980. *Der Kriminalroman.* Stuttgart: Metzler.

Oatley, Keith. 1994. "A Taxonomy of the Emotions of Literary Response and a Theory of Identification in Fictional Narrative." *Poetics* 23:53–74.

O'Neill, Patrick. 2005. "Narrative Structure." In *The Routledge Encyclopedia of Narrative Theory,* ed. David Herman, Manfred Jahn, and Marie-Laure Ryan, 366–70. London: Routledge.

Ortega y Gasset, José. 1948. *The Dehumanization of Art and Notes on the Novel.* Princeton, N.J.: Princeton University Press. (Orig. pub. 1929.)

Paivio, Allan. 1983. "The Mind's Eye in Arts and Science." *Poetics* 12:1–18.

Pavel, Thomas. 1986. *Fictional Worlds.* Cambridge, Mass.: Harvard University Press.

———. 2006. "The Novel in Search of Itself: A Historical Morphology." In *The Novel.* Vol. 2 of *Forms and Themes,* ed. Franco Moretti, 3–31. Princeton, N.J.: Princeton University Press.

Pearce, Lynn. 1994. *Reading Dialogics.* London: Arnold.

Piaget, Jean, 1967. "Les Données génétiques de l'épistémologie physique." In *Encyclopédie de la Pléiade: Logique et connaissance scientifique,*ed. Jean Piaget, 599–622. Paris: Gallimard.

Pleij, Herman. 1997. *Dromen van Cocagne: Middeleeuwse fantasieën over het volmaakte leven.* Amsterdam: Prometheus.

Poole, Brian. 1998. "Bakhtin and Cassirer: The Philosophical Origins of Bakhtin's Carnival Messianism." *South Atlantic Quarterly* 97:579–98.

Prigogine, Ilya. 1984. "De tijd herontdekken." *Tijd: De vierde dimensie in de kunst,* ed. Michel Baudson, 23–33. Brussels: Vereniging voor tentoonstellingen van het Paleis voor Schone Kunsten Brussel.

Prince, Gerald. 1982. *Narratology: The Form and Functioning of Narrative.* Berlin and New York: Mouton.

Propp, Vladmir. 1997. *De morfologie van het toversprookje: Vormleer van een genre.* Vert. door Max Louwerse. Utrecht: Spectrum.

Rabinowitz, Peter. 2002. "Reading Beginnings and Endings." In *Narrative Dynamics: Essays on Time, Plot, Closure, and Frames,* ed. Brian Richardson, 300–312. Columbus: Ohio State University Press.

Radway, Janice. 1984. *Reading the Romance: Women, Patriarchy, and Popular Literature.* London: Verso.

Richardson, Brian. 2005. "Causality." In *The Routledge Encyclopedia of Narrative Theory,* ed. David Herman, Manfred Jahn, and Marie-Laure Ryan, 48–52. London: Routledge.

Richter, David H. 1994. *The Progress of Romance: Literary Historiography and the Gothic Novel.* Columbus: Ohio State University Press.

Ricoeur, Paul. 1984. *Temps et récit II: La configuration du temps dans le récit de fiction.* Paris: Seuil.

Ryan, Marie-Laure. 1991. *Possible Worlds, Artificial Intelligence, and Narrative Theory.* Bloomington: Indiana University Press.

————. 2003a. "Cognitive Maps and the Construction of Narrative Space." In *Narrative Theory and the Cognitive Sciences,* ed. David Herman, 214–42. Stanford, Calif.: Publications of the Center for the Study of Language and Information.

————. 2003b. "Narrative Cartography: Toward a Visual Narratology." In *What Is Narratology?,* ed. Tom Kindt, 333–64. Berlin: De Gruyter.

Ryle, Gilbert. 1990. *The Concept of Mind.* Harmondsworth: Penguin. (Orig. pub. 1968.)

Schank, Roger C. 1982. *Dynamic Memory: A Theory of Reminding and Learning in Computers and People.* Cambridge: Cambridge University Press.

Schank, Roger, and R. P. Abelson. 1977. *Scripts, Plans, Goals and Understanding: An Inquiry into Human Knowledge Structures.* Hillsdale, N.J.: Lawrence Erlbaum Associates.

Schipper, Mineke. 1999. *Het zwarte paradijs Afrikaanse scheppingsmythen.* Rijswijk: Elmar.

Schmidt, Siegfried J. 1984. "The Fiction Is That Reality Exists: A Constructivist Model of Reality, Fiction, and Literature." *Poetics Today* 2:253–74.

Schopenhauer, Arthur. 1969. "Appendix: Criticism of the Kantian Philosophy." In vol. 1 of *The World as Will and Representation.* New York: Dover Press.

Shusterman, Richard. 2001. "Art as Dramatization." *Journal of Aesthetics and Art Criticism* 59 (4): 363–72.

Simons, Anton. 1996. *Carnaval en terreur: De ethische betekenis van Bakhtins rable.* Enschede: Ipskamp.

Sophocles. 2006. *Oedipus the King.* Project Gutenberg. http://www.gutenberg.org/files/31/31-h/31-h.htm/ (accessed April 26, 2010).

Suvin, Darko. 1985. "On Metaphoricity and Narrativity in Fiction: The Chronotope as the Differentia Generica." *SubStance* 48. http://www.arts.uwo.ca/substance/48/suvin.html/ (accessed January 2, 2007; site now discontinued).

————. 1989. "The Chronotope, Possible Worlds and Narrativity." In vol. 2 of *Narratologie, texte, genre: Proceedings of the XIth ICLA-Conference,* ed. Jean Bessière, 33–41. New York: Peter Lang.

Sztranyiczki, Zsófia. 2006. "Spatio-temporality in Narrative Fiction: Humboldt's Gift by Saul Bellow." *Argumentum* 2:1–16.

Ten Kate, Laurens, and Jean-Luc Nancy. 2010. "Cum Revisited: Some Preliminaries to Thinking the Interval." *Intermedialities: Theory, History, Performance,* ed. Henk Oosterling and Eva Ziarek (forthcoming). http://www.uvh.nl/uploadeddocumenten/cumrevisited.pdf/ (accessed April 26, 2010).

Thorndyke, Perry W., and Frank R. Yekovich. 1980. "A Critique of Schema-Based Theories of Human Story Memory." *Poetics* 9:23–49.

Todorov, Tzvetan. 1968. "La grammaire du récit." *Languages* 12:94–102. http://www.persee.fr/web/revues/home/prescript/article/lgge_0458-726x_1968_num_3_12_2355/ (accessed April 26, 2010).

———. 1969. *La Grammaire du Décaméron.* La Haye: Mouton.

Van Dijk, Teun A. 1977. "Semantic Macro-structures and Knowledge Frames in Discourse Comprehension." In *Cognitive Processes in Comprehension*, ed. P. A. Carpenter and M. A. Just, 3–32. Hillsdale, N.J.: Lawrence Erlbaum Associates.

Van Dijk, Teun A., and Walter Kintsch. 1983. *Strategies of Text Comprehension.* New York: Academic Press.

Van Gennep, Arnold. 1960. *The Rites of Passage.* Trans. Monika B. Vizedom and Gabrielle L. Caffee. London: Routledge. (Orig. pub. 1909.)

Van Gorp, Hendrik. 1978. *Inleiding tot de picareske verhaalkunst of de wederwaardigheden van een anti-genre.* Groningen: Wolters-Noordhoff.

———. 1998. *De romantische griezelroman (Gothic Novel): Een merkwaardig rand-verschijnsel in de literatuur.* Leuven: Garant.

Van Luxemburg, Jan en W. G. Weststeijn. 1983. *Inleiding in de literatuurwetenschap.* Muiderberg: Coutinho. (Orig. pub. 1981.)

Vernant, Jean-Pierre. 1963. "Sur l'expression religieuse de l'espace et du mouvement chez les Grecs." *L'Homme: Revue française d'anthropologie* 3:12–50.

Vlasov, Eduard. 1995. "The World According to Bakhtin: On the Description of Space and Spatial Forms in Mikhail Bakhtin's Works." *Canadian Slavonic Papers* 37 (1–2): 37–58.

Voloshinov, V. N. 1983. "Discourse in Life and Discourse in Poetry: Questions of Sociological Poetics." In *Bakhtin School Papers (Russian Poetics in Translation 10)*, ed. Ann Shukman, 5–30. Oxford: RPT. (Orig. pub. 1926.)

Watt, Ian. 1957. *The Rise of the Novel: Studies in Defoe, Richardson, and Fielding.* London: Hogarth Press.

Weisgerber, Jean. 1978. *L'Espace Romanesque.* Lausanne: L'Age d'Homme.

Wellek, René, and Austin Warren. 1976. *Theory of Literature.* Harmondsworth: Penguin Books. (Orig. pub. 1942.)

White, E. C. 1987. *Kaironomia: On the Will-to-Invent.* Ithaca, N.Y.: Cornell University Press.

Wilson, Edward O. 1978. *On Human Nature.* Cambridge, Mass.: Harvard University Press.

Wilson, Rawdon. 1995. "The Metamorphoses of Fictional Space: Magical Realism."

In *Magical Realism: Theory, History, Community,* ed. Lois Parkinson Zamora and Wendy B. Faris, 209–34. Durham, N.C.: Duke University Press.

Zmegac, Victor. 1991. *Der Europäische Roman: Geschichte seiner Poetik.* Tübingen: Niemeyer.

Zoran, Gabriel. 1984. "Towards a Theory of Space in Narrative." *Poetics Today* 5 (2): 309–35.

Index

About the Author

Bart Keunen is a professor of comparative literature at Ghent University in Belgium.